Llewellyn's

D1445836

Witches' Datebook

2020

Featuring

Art by Jennifer Hewitson
Text by Elizabeth Barrette, Danielle Blackwood,
Emily Carlin, Anna Franklin, James Kambos,
Barbara Moore, Melissa Tipton, Tess Whitehurst,
Charlie Rainbow Wolf, and Laura Tempest Zakroff

ISBN 978-0-7387-4953-2

2020

JANUARY
S	M	T	W	T	F	S
			1	2	3	4
5	6	7	8	9	10	11
12	13	14	15	16	17	18
19	20	21	22	23	24	25
26	27	28	29	30	31	

FEBRUARY
S	M	T	W	T	F	S
						1
2	3	4	5	6	7	8
9	10	11	12	13	14	15
16	17	18	19	20	21	22
23	24	25	26	27	28	29

MARCH
S	M	T	W	T	F	S
1	2	3	4	5	6	7
8	9	10	11	12	13	14
15	16	17	18	19	20	21
22	23	24	25	26	27	28
29	30	31				

APRIL
S	M	T	W	T	F	S
			1	2	3	4
5	6	7	8	9	10	11
12	13	14	15	16	17	18
19	20	21	22	23	24	25
26	27	28	29	30		

MAY
S	M	T	W	T	F	S
					1	2
3	4	5	6	7	8	9
10	11	12	13	14	15	16
17	18	19	20	21	22	23
24	25	26	27	28	29	30
31						

JUNE
S	M	T	W	T	F	S
	1	2	3	4	5	6
7	8	9	10	11	12	13
14	15	16	17	18	19	20
21	22	23	24	25	26	27
28	29	30				

JULY
S	M	T	W	T	F	S
			1	2	3	4
5	6	7	8	9	10	11
12	13	14	15	16	17	18
19	20	21	22	23	24	25
26	27	28	29	30	31	

AUGUST
S	M	T	W	T	F	S
						1
2	3	4	5	6	7	8
9	10	11	12	13	14	15
16	17	18	19	20	21	22
23	24	25	26	27	28	29
30	31					

SEPTEMBER
S	M	T	W	T	F	S
		1	2	3	4	5
6	7	8	9	10	11	12
13	14	15	16	17	18	19
20	21	22	23	24	25	26
27	28	29	30			

OCTOBER
S	M	T	W	T	F	S
				1	2	3
4	5	6	7	8	9	10
11	12	13	14	15	16	17
18	19	20	21	22	23	24
25	26	27	28	29	30	31

NOVEMBER
S	M	T	W	T	F	S
1	2	3	4	5	6	7
8	9	10	11	12	13	14
15	16	17	18	19	20	21
22	23	24	25	26	27	28
29	30					

DECEMBER
S	M	T	W	T	F	S
		1	2	3	4	5
6	7	8	9	10	11	12
13	14	15	16	17	18	19
20	21	22	23	24	25	26
27	28	29	30	31		

2021

JANUARY
S	M	T	W	T	F	S
					1	2
3	4	5	6	7	8	9
10	11	12	13	14	15	16
17	18	19	20	21	22	23
24	25	26	27	28	29	30
31						

FEBRUARY
S	M	T	W	T	F	S
	1	2	3	4	5	6
7	8	9	10	11	12	13
14	15	16	17	18	19	20
21	22	23	24	25	26	27
28						

MARCH
S	M	T	W	T	F	S
	1	2	3	4	5	6
7	8	9	10	11	12	13
14	15	16	17	18	19	20
21	22	23	24	25	26	27
28	29	30	31			

APRIL
S	M	T	W	T	F	S
				1	2	3
4	5	6	7	8	9	10
11	12	13	14	15	16	17
18	19	20	21	22	23	24
25	26	27	28	29	30	

MAY
S	M	T	W	T	F	S
						1
2	3	4	5	6	7	8
9	10	11	12	13	14	15
16	17	18	19	20	21	22
23	24	25	26	27	28	29
30	31					

JUNE
S	M	T	W	T	F	S
		1	2	3	4	5
6	7	8	9	10	11	12
13	14	15	16	17	18	19
20	21	22	23	24	25	26
27	28	29	30			

JULY
S	M	T	W	T	F	S
				1	2	3
4	5	6	7	8	9	10
11	12	13	14	15	16	17
18	19	20	21	22	23	24
25	26	27	28	29	30	31

AUGUST
S	M	T	W	T	F	S
1	2	3	4	5	6	7
8	9	10	11	12	13	14
15	16	17	18	19	20	21
22	23	24	25	26	27	28
29	30	31				

SEPTEMBER
S	M	T	W	T	F	S
			1	2	3	4
5	6	7	8	9	10	11
12	13	14	15	16	17	18
19	20	21	22	23	24	25
26	27	28	29	30		

OCTOBER
S	M	T	W	T	F	S
					1	2
3	4	5	6	7	8	9
10	11	12	13	14	15	16
17	18	19	20	21	22	23
24	25	26	27	28	29	30
31						

NOVEMBER
S	M	T	W	T	F	S
	1	2	3	4	5	6
7	8	9	10	11	12	13
14	15	16	17	18	19	20
21	22	23	24	25	26	27
28	29	30				

DECEMBER
S	M	T	W	T	F	S
			1	2	3	4
5	6	7	8	9	10	11
12	13	14	15	16	17	18
19	20	21	22	23	24	25
26	27	28	29	30	31	

Editing and layout by Lauryn Heineman

Cover illustration and interior art © 2019 by Jennifer Hewitson

Art on chapter openings © 2006 by Jennifer Hewitson

Art direction by Lynne Menturweck

Table of Contents

How to Use Llewellyn's Witches' Datebook

Welcome to *Llewellyn's 2020 Witches' Datebook*! This datebook was designed especially for Witches, Pagans, and magical people. Use it to plan sabbat celebrations, magic, Full Moon rites, and even dentist and doctor appointments. At right is a symbol key to some of the features of this datebook.

MOON QUARTERS: The Moon's cycle is divided into four quarters, which are noted in the weekly pages along with their exact times. When the Moon changes quarter, both quarters are listed, as well as the time of the change. In addition, a symbol for the new quarter is placed where the numeral for the date usually appears.

MOON IN THE SIGNS: Approximately every two and a half days, the Moon moves from one zodiac sign to the next. The sign that the Moon is in at the beginning of the day (midnight Eastern Time) is noted next to the quarter listing. If the Moon changes signs that day, there will be a notation saying "☽ enters" followed by the symbol for the sign it is entering.

MOON VOID-OF-COURSE: Just before the Moon enters a new sign, it will make one final aspect (angular relationship) to another planet. Between that last aspect and the entrance of the Moon into the next sign it is said to be void-of-course. Activities begun when the Moon is void-of-course rarely come to fruition, or they turn out very differently than planned.

4

PLANETARY MOVEMENT: When a planet or asteroid moves from one sign into another, this change (called an *ingress*) is noted on the calendar pages with the exact time. The Moon and Sun are considered planets in this case. The planets (except for the Sun and Moon) can also appear to move backward as seen from the Earth. This is called a *planetary retrograde*, and is noted on the calendar pages with the symbol ℞. When the planet begins to move forward, or direct, again, it is marked D, and the time is also noted.

PLANTING AND HARVESTING DAYS: The best days for planting and harvesting are noted on the calendar pages with a seedling icon (planting) and a basket icon (harvesting).

TIME ZONE CHANGES: The times and dates of all astrological phenomena in this datebook are based on Eastern time. If you live outside the Eastern time zone, you will need to make the following changes: Pacific Time subtract three hours; Mountain Time subtract two hours; Central Time subtract one hour; Alaska subtract four hours; and Hawaii subtract five hours. All data is adjusted for Daylight Saving Time.

Planets

☉	Sun	♅	Uranus
☽	Moon	♆	Neptune
☿	Mercury	♇	Pluto
♀	Venus	⚷	Chiron
♂	Mars		
♃	Jupiter		
♄	Saturn		

Signs

♈	Aries	♐	Sagittarius
♉	Taurus	♑	Capricorn
♊	Gemini	♒	Aquarius
♋	Cancer	♓	Pisces
♌	Leo		
♍	Virgo		
♎	Libra		
♏	Scorpio		

Motion

℞ Retrograde
D Direct

1st Quarter/New Moon ☽
2nd Quarter ○

3rd Quarter/Full Moon ☺
4th Quarter ○

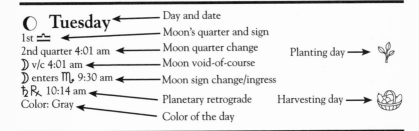

○ **Tuesday** ← Day and date
1st ♎ ← Moon's quarter and sign
2nd quarter 4:01 am ← Moon quarter change   Planting day → 🌱
☽ v/c 4:01 am ← Moon void-of-course
☽ enters ♏ 9:30 am ← Moon sign change/ingress
♄ ℞ 10:14 am ← Planetary retrograde   Harvesting day → 🧺
Color: Gray ← Color of the day

5

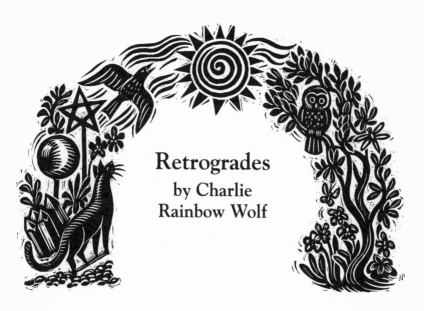

Retrogrades
by Charlie Rainbow Wolf

You're probably familiar with Mercury retrograde because it happens so often, but did you know that all the planets have a retrograde period? The only exceptions to this are the Sun, because it's the star all the planets orbit; the Moon, because it's Earth's satellite; and the Earth—although if you visited another planet, then you'd see the Earth travel backward! Retrograde doesn't mean that the planet actually reverses its orbit; it's an optical illusion that makes it appear this way.

Venus

Venus is the planet of love, balance, and harmony. Its retrograde is the rarest, occurring approximately every eighteen months and lasting around six weeks. This year it enters the retrograde zone in April at 5° Gemini, stations in May at 21° Gemini, and continues the backward dance until the end of June, when it stations direct at 5° Gemini, leaving its shadow period the end of July.

This isn't the best time to start a summer romance or spend big money. Temptations are strong and willpower is weak. Your natural perception of what is sensible is on hold while overindulgence tries—and often succeeds—to overpower it. Those expensive shoes might not look so appealing once the retrograde period finishes. The same goes for romances: the perfect match might turn out to be a dud once Venus starts moving forward again.

Mercury

Mercury is associated with communication and travel. Mercury retrogrades most frequently, around three times a year. They don't last long, somewhere in the region of three weeks. Mercury starts its backward dance in February, June, and October this year. Factor in the astrological signs and the shadow periods when planning important meetings or making travel plans.

Mercury retrograde messes with technology—anything from online communication to schedules and transit. It's easy to misplace something, miss a connection, or be involved in misunderstandings during this period. This sounds like a downer, but it's also a great time to review your progress and evaluate your priorities. Reconnections with people from your past often happen when Mercury is retrograde, but don't rekindle that relationship before rethinking what you hope to achieve!

Mars

Mars is pretty volatile to begin with, and the retrograde period makes things even more unsettled. Mars is associated with adventure, assertiveness, and action. Mars retrograde only comes around every couple of years, making it the second-rarest retrograde, and lasts just over two months. It enters the retrograde zone in late July, stations in September, turns direct in November, and clears its shadow the first week of 2021.

You'll feel impatient during this period, but it's not a time to rush forward into anything. You might be more accident prone than usual—another reason to take your time. If you're easily upset, this is an ideal period to seek help or counseling. If you use this time to your advantage, you'll be able to come to terms with whatever issues the retrograde period exposes and take the appropriate action. Then, once Mars moves out of its shadow period, you're also moving forward toward your goals.

The Outer Planets

I believe the retrogrades of the outer planets have less of an impact than those of the inner planets. There are exceptions to this, and the first of those is if the planets are making strong aspects—geometric angles—to other planets in the sky at the same time. The second exception is if the planet is aspecting a planet or power point in your natal birth chart. The outer planets move slowly and tend to bring about slow evolution, unlike the inner planet transits, which tend to be more fleeting things. The outer planets go retrograde for several months every year. Aside from the aforementioned conditions, their strongest influence will be when they change stations.

Jupiter

Jupiter is the planet of luck and abundance, and this is true even during the retrograde period. In fact, the retrograde often benefits Jupiter. It's a wonderful time for reflection and philosophical contemplation. Lessons to help you to find your authentic self come your way to set you up for reaching your full potential, if you let them. Jupiter's backward dance brings a chance to determine what's really important and where you're merely distracted. It's a time for overcoming self-indulgence and breaking habits, so when Jupiter turns direct, the new and improved you is ready to seize every opportunity that comes your way.

Saturn

Saturn often gets a bad rap as the "Lord of Karma" or "The Great Malefic." Saturn is only a problem if you've been trying to cut corners and shirk your responsibility. It's a great disciplinarian, which is why some people dread its aspects, but let me ask you this: What loving father doesn't discipline his child?

Saturn retrogrades and Saturn returns can be a bit tricky, especially when one overlaps the other. Saturn's orbit is twenty-nine years, so your Saturn return comes around at twenty-nine, fifty-eight, and, if you're lucky, eighty-seven. If one of those is your age in 2020, then this retrograde applies particularly to you! It starts entering its shadow at 25° Capricorn but doesn't station retrograde until May, at nearly 2° Aquarius. The "old man" stations direct the end of September but won't actually leave the retrograde zone until 2021.

The most important days of this retrograde are when it hits the anoretic degree of 29° Capricorn the second week in March of this year and then again the first half of July. Those are likely to be the most rocky days, the days when things just feel out of sorts or don't seem to be happening. This is particularly important because Saturn and Pluto are going to be conjunct in Capricorn on and off for most

of the year, frequently bumped
into by Jupiter, and joined by
Mars in February and March. Saturn's pretty happy at home here
in Capricorn, but Jupiter doesn't
like the restrictive energy at all.
At least Mars likes the sign of the
"old goat"!

I've waffled on about Saturn
a bit because this is an important transit, particularly if it dings
one of your natal power points
or planets. You may feel limited,
particularly when it comes to shouldering too many responsibilities or
feeling that others depend on you too much. Take extra time these
days and don't lose your cool with Mars's energy or Jupiter's frustra-
tions. Look at the areas of your life that you want to work on and bring
into balance, for Saturn's retrograde will give you a chance to do just
that. It's all about responsibility. Hard work, yes, but it comes with such
high reward!

Uranus

If you want to know why your life has suddenly started to feel like it is
full of unexpected changes, look to see what Uranus is doing! When
you're affected by Uranus's retrograde, it's harder to focus and you're
more changeable than usual. How this will impact you depends on
where the retrograde lands in your chart. Uranus retrograde in Taurus
tends to be a bit uncomfortable, for they don't have much in common.
Uranus is impulsive and rebellious, but Taurus is methodical and seeks
security. Uranus is going to be in Taurus until 2026, so there's time to
learn how to work with, rather than against, the retrogrades as they
occur.

Neptune

Neptune is home in Pisces now and for several more years, and it's quite
happy in this position. Its movements influence your hopes and dreams,
your spiritual evolution, and potential attachment issues. When Neptune retrogrades, it's easy for phobias and fears to surface. If you've been
deluding yourself in any way, those illusions could be shattered, exposing
the truth. The deeper your fantasies, the harsher the truth might appear,

especially if you've been self-medicating in some way. However rough or painful it might appear, exposing the truth is always a good thing, for it helps you embrace your higher self and grow your soul.

Pluto

First it is a planet, then it is no planet, then it is!* Pluto is farthest from the Earth, so its retrogrades pass largely unnoticed, apart from if they impact you personally or are part of an important aspect pattern. Pluto is associated with evolution, like the phoenix, who dies and rises from the ashes. Look to Pluto to find your personal transformation, where you need to let go and grow, and what is holding you back from being all you can be. Pluto's retrograde is a time when you may be forced to come to terms with things, demolishing what has power over you, so you once again can take control of your destiny.

Conclusion

Some people believe retrogrades are detrimental. I don't think that's necessarily true; however, anything can seem negative if you're naturally pessimistic! A planet's retrograde inhibits its energy, limits its potential, and perhaps creates some delays or disruption. Retrogrades are a wonderful time for all the *re-* words, like review, reorganize, reflect, revamp, revise, and more. Use them to your advantage!

*Paraphrase of Zen proverb.

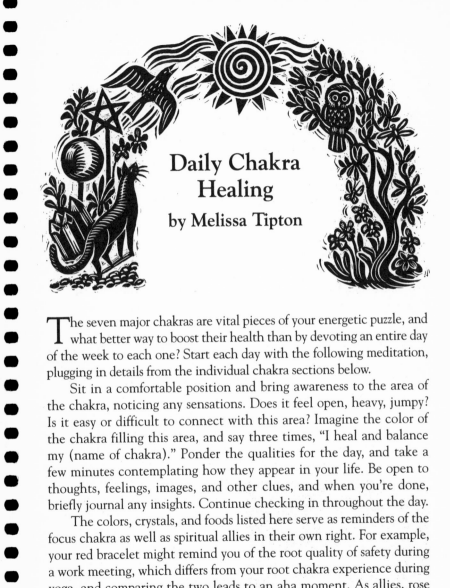

Daily Chakra Healing
by Melissa Tipton

The seven major chakras are vital pieces of your energetic puzzle, and what better way to boost their health than by devoting an entire day of the week to each one? Start each day with the following meditation, plugging in details from the individual chakra sections below.

Sit in a comfortable position and bring awareness to the area of the chakra, noticing any sensations. Does it feel open, heavy, jumpy? Is it easy or difficult to connect with this area? Imagine the color of the chakra filling this area, and say three times, "I heal and balance my (name of chakra)." Ponder the qualities for the day, and take a few minutes contemplating how they appear in your life. Be open to thoughts, feelings, images, and other clues, and when you're done, briefly journal any insights. Continue checking in throughout the day.

The colors, crystals, and foods listed here serve as reminders of the focus chakra as well as spiritual allies in their own right. For example, your red bracelet might remind you of the root quality of safety during a work meeting, which differs from your root chakra experience during yoga, and comparing the two leads to an aha moment. As allies, rose quartz could trigger heart chakra insights, while a sniff of rosemary might bring to mind an important memory in relation to your solar plexus. Keep in mind that this is less about isolating definitive answers and more about letting one question lead you to the next, like spiritual breadcrumbs that take you deeper into self-awareness.

11

Monday: Root

Today's focus is safety and its shadow side, stagnation. This chakra helps us cultivate the foundation necessary to survive and thrive, and without this stable base, it's challenging to manifest what we need. We might feel as if we're taking one step forward and two steps back, never able to gain a solid footing. On the flip side, we can become so attached to stability and supports that they become constraints, preventing us from evolving and remaining flexible. Today, get curious about where you feel safe or unsafe (physically, emotionally, spiritually, or intellectually) and where you feel stuck. If you imagined breaking free from stagnation, what might that look like, and what thoughts and feelings arise?

Color: Red

Location: Base of the spine

Crystals (wear, carry, or meditate with): Garnet, hematite, red calcite, jasper

Food and Drink: Red potatoes, red beans or lentils, radishes, beets, rooibos or hibiscus teas, dandelion root tea for deep grounding

Tuesday: Navel

Today's focus is vulnerability versus naïveté. Vulnerability is often viewed as a weakness, but in truth it's a superpower founded in trusting that our authentic expression is valuable and necessary. Vulnerability asks us to reveal who we really are, not a pared-down persona; it's the act of giving ourselves permission to be ourselves. When we try to be what we are not, we lose touch with those gut feelings that steer us away from needlessly harmful situations. The navel helps discern between exposing the true self to enable authentic expression and

 intimacy versus sticking our head in the sand and exposing ourselves to danger. Get curious about areas where you're pressuring yourself to adopt a persona, people please, or otherwise keep your true nature under wraps as well as areas where you might be overriding inner alarm bells—are there connections between the two?

Color: Orange

Location: Just below the belly button

Crystals: Amber, carnelian, peach moonstone, orange calcite
Food and Drink: Carrots, orange peppers, oranges, calendula tea with
    orange peel and a pinch of turmeric

Wednesday: Solar Plexus

Today's focus is responsibility versus control and the interesting, often inverse, relationship between the two. Controlling behavior, whether directed at ourselves or others, often conceals unconscious responsibilities that must be owned if the controlling patterns are to be healed. For example, if you struggle with micromanaging your diet, this could conceal a need to own your emotions and embodied experiences. It can feel easier to hyperfocus on controllable factors, like what to eat and how much, instead of exploring the messier emotions surrounding those food choices. Today, get curious about aspects of your life that feel controlled or overly rule-bound. What feelings come up when you ponder loosening the reins? Can you take responsibility simply by being fully present with the feelings, and if they reveal a need for change, how can you take the next step in that direction?

Color: Yellow
Location: Upper abdomen
Crystals: Citrine, topaz, yellow tiger's eye, sunstone
Food and Drink: Bananas, melons, olive oil, cinnamon, rosemary,
    chamomile tea, water with lemon juice

Thursday: Heart

Today's focus is abundance versus hoarding. The heart is the great connector between the chakras as the midpoint of these seven energy centers and between us and all of life. When the chakras are healthy, the heart has the support of the entire system, enjoying, for example, the safety of the root and the vulnerability of the navel, which allow the heart to remain open and connected. This connection helps us perceive opportunities and support, and this generates trust that we will have enough without hoarding. Today, get curious about areas of anxiety and worry, areas where you feel like you have to hold on or prevent change for fear of loss. Can you sit with your uncomfortable feelings while simultaneously tapping into self-love? Shower yourself with green or pink light and bathe your worries in love. Does the addition of heart energy give you a glimpse of previously hidden options or ideas, and if so, can you take the next step toward them?

Color: Green or pink

Location: Center of the chest

Crystals: Emerald, rose quartz, peridot, green kyanite

Food and Drink: Green and red foods, such as a salad of leafy greens
with sweet apple slices and raw pumpkin seeds; tonic of aloe vera
juice; herbals teas with hawthorn, rose, or jasmine

Friday: Throat

Today's focus is productive dialogue versus monologue, both internally
and with others. Dialogue invites new perspectives and requires flexi-
bility, while monologue sticks to the script and is immune to change.
Our thoughts can remain open and curious or resist new perspectives.
In conversation, we can allow ourselves to be surprised, to truly listen
and be present, or we can wait for our turn to resume our monologue.
Notice how dialogue builds on the previous chakras: for example, we're
more apt to welcome change and surprises when we feel safe (root),
and we're less likely to make negative assumptions when we feel connected (heart). Both feelings foster healthy dialogue over fearful, rigid
monologue. Today, practice being present and curious in conversations,
whether they're happening internally or with others. When your mind
is certain, say, "I wonder what other possibilities exist—I'm open to
perceiving them." Be fully present in conversation. Don't worry about
what you're going to say next; simply savor the details, said and unsaid.

Color: Sky blue

Location: Base of the throat

Crystals: Lapis, sodalite, celestine, blue kyanite

Food and Drink: Blueberries, blackberries, plums (blend them into a
yummy smoothie); throat-soothing broths; teas with red clover,
lemon balm, slippery elm, or marshmallow root

Saturday: Third Eye

Today's focus is intuition versus fantasy: what is true versus what we
want to be true. Intuition can be firm and, at times, quite loud, but
it's never panicked or in a rush, even when change is long past due.
Fantasy, however, sweeps in with grand visions that have an urgency
borne from the belief that this idea is the ticket—the diet, the career
change, the whatever that will finally create desired change. Fantasy is
often packaged with fear of missing out if we don't jump on its advice,
so today, get curious about your inner dialogue and feelings. If you're
moved to pursue a course of action, what feelings and thoughts arise if

you consider not doing so? When we ignore our intuition, we might feel a heaviness or dullness, as if some of the life has been drained from us, whereas thwarting our fantasies can trigger anxiety and the pressure to charge forward, no matter the cost.

Color: Indigo
Location: Between the brows
Crystals: Lapis, amethyst, fluorite, tanzanite, indigo gabbro
Food and Drink: Goji berries, eggplant, purple cabbage coleslaw, plums, plenty of water, açai or sparkling grape juice, eyebright tea

Sunday: Crown

Today's focus is surrender versus escapism. The Divine works through us, not for us; we must serve as responsible cocreators of our life. Too often surrender is interpreted as a come-what-may approach, but there's more nuance to healthy surrender. What must be released are the rigid plans of the ego in favor of trusting that taking the next step is enough. Once that step is initiated, we will be given the next, but we won't be shown the entire map before we agree to leave the house, nor can we escape the responsibility of taking action in the absence of complete knowledge. This is the dance of surrender. Today, explore your plans and goals. Do you have any? Are they set in stone? Pare it down to just the next step, asking for guidance and allowing your intuition to inform you actions. If you're guided to a follow-up step that deviates from the ego's plans, can you surrender, taking action with openness and curiosity?

Color: White or purple
Location: At or just above the top of the head
Crystals: Herkimer diamond, quartz, selenite, moonstone
Food and Drink: Yogurt and kefir; nuts and seeds, especially almond and sesame; sea salt; lavender or lotus tea

Pop Culture Protection Magick
by Emily Carlin

It's a big, scary world out there, and it isn't always kind. Sometimes you're strong and fortified and ready to face whatever life can dish out, and sometimes you're not. Sometimes you feel damaged and vulnerable, too vulnerable to deal with the world at large alone. Thankfully, as a magickal practitioner, you never have to. Using pop culture magick, you can turn your favorite fictional character into a metaphysical bodyguard to watch over you, protect you from incoming threats, and help you deal with negative energies that you encounter.

There are as many forms of pop culture magick as there are practitioners, multiplied by the amount of pop culture available to them—so rather a lot, to put it mildly. We'll focus on character-driven pop culture magick, in which pop culture characters are treated as preexisting thought forms on the astral plane. If you have not worked with pop culture characters before, try to think of them as being similar to fae or spirits: they are unique individuals with their own personalities and have varying abilities to act in our world. The power these characters are able to exert depends on both their intrinsic power (how much energy the popular conscious has poured into them over the years and how popular they are at any given time) and the strength of your connection to them. As with any other metaphysical entity, pop culture characters can be worked with in a multitude of ways, including for protection magic.

Do you like superheros, rogues, wizards, soldiers, adventurers, or antiheroes? Do you prefer character from movies, television, books, comics, video games, role playing, or somewhere else entirely? Take a moment to think of your favorite pop culture characters who have protective traits and imagine what it would be like to have them accompany you throughout your day, helping you face your challenges and keeping you safe. That is what pop culture protectors do. You can think of them as metaphysical bodyguards. Their job is to watch over you, protect

you from incoming threats, and help you deal with negative energies you encounter.

There are several qualities that make characters more or less suitable for work as protectors. First and foremost is your relationship with that character. How well do you know the character? Have you worked with them before? Energetically engaging with a character over time (watching your favorite movies and TV shows, reading books, wearing fandom T-shirts, engaging with other fans, doing magick, etc.) forges a metaphysical connection between you and that character. As with any metaphysical entity, the stronger the energetic connection the easier it will be to work with that character magickally. Workings become both easier and more effective when they align with the existing values and goals of the character. Asking Captain America to help you defend yourself from bullies is likely to be much more productive than asking him to help you rob a bank. The former is perfectly aligned with his known values and the latter is explicitly against them. By choosing to work with a character who supports your goals, you save yourself a lot of arm-twisting, regardless of the strength of your relationship with that character. Always try to work with characters you have strong relationships with and whose values and goals are in alignment with the intent of your working.

A character you have a strong and healthy relationship with will always be better for protective work than one you don't know well, even if your character isn't, at first glance, intrinsically protective. Obvious protectors are warrior characters—think superheroes, soldiers, most video game protagonists, and the like—for whom physical defense is integral to the character. Sorcerers, witches, and other magickal fighters

are also fairly obvious protectors—think Gandalf, Glinda, Dr. Strange, and so on—as they have the power to go up against almost any foe. However, a character doesn't need to wield fireballs, swords, or guns to be an effective protector. Just like regular people, pop culture characters will perform astonishing feats of strength to protect those they care for. Further, the support of a friend is often more effective against negativity than any barrier. It would be better to have Molly Weasley as a protector than Conan the Barbarian, despite his perceived strengths versus hers, if you have a relationship with Molly and not with Conan. Add to that Molly's ferocity when it comes to defending those she cares about, and the choice is easy. Conversely, regardless of your relationship with them, it would be unwise to choose particularly selfish or chaotic characters as protectors, as they cannot be consistently relied upon to protect others.

The second qualities to look at are a character's resilience and adaptability. Unless your chosen character is accustomed to navigating tricky situations in the mundane world (think Jessica Jones or James Bond), they will need to adapt to the role of protector. Some characters, while brilliant in their own environment, either aren't terribly suited for navigating the mundane or just aren't energetically vigorous enough to deal with the energies most people have to deal with day to day. A delicate flower fairy can be a lovely and supportive companion; however, they aren't exactly going to take down a hellhound. Characters like Hermione Granger, Ant Man, and Jyn Erso are much better at rolling with whatever life may toss your way. To be effective, a protector must be able to navigate the world in way that inspires confidence and a feeling of safety.

Another important factor is the situation in which you find yourself. If you know ahead of time what type of energies or antagonists you're likely to deal with, you can choose protectors best suited to the problems at hand. If you need help dealing with a school or work environment, choose a character who does particularly well there: for example, Professor X or Pepper Potts. If you know you'll need to deal with family difficulties, perhaps choose Aunt May or Wilfred Mott

(Donna's grandfather from *Doctor Who*). If you don't know what you may face, a general protector will always help.

Once you've selected a character you would like as a protector, you must ask if they are willing to act on your behalf. A protector must choose you as much as you choose them; a reluctant or coerced protector is ineffective at best and obstructive at worst. Call on the character and explicitly set out the reasons you'd like the character to be your protector, where you'd like them to accompany you, and for how long. You can do this by having a conversation through a divination tool, ritual, and so on—whatever metaphysical communication method you find most effective. Depending on the character, you may be asked to give a specific offering or perform an act of gratitude in exchange for their help. Do feel free to negotiate reasonable terms; you're not required to do anything you're uncomfortable with. If you and the character come to an agreement, then you're good to go. If not, choose another character and begin the process again. As stated previously, an unwilling protector is often worse than no protector at all.

Just as you would show your gratitude to anyone who helped you in the mundane, it is good manners to show your appreciation to the metaphysical entities that aid you. After the agreed time frame of protection has finished (or periodically, if it's ongoing), be sure to properly thank your protector. Just as mundane friends don't often require elaborate thanks due to the constant exchange of gratitude and affection, neither do many pop culture entities. If you work with the character regularly, the act may be as simple as just saying thank you out loud. The less well you know the entity the grander a gesture of thanks is often required, as they've come and done you a favor either in exchange for a promise of some sort or on faith that you'd be gracious about it. Once thanks are given and promises fulfilled, you may dismiss the entity however you usually do so.

Pop culture protectors are a wonderful way to fortify yourself against a wide variety of negative entities and energies. By creating relationships with strong pop culture characters, you arm yourself with the magickal resilience needed to rise to any challenge and navigate the world successfully.

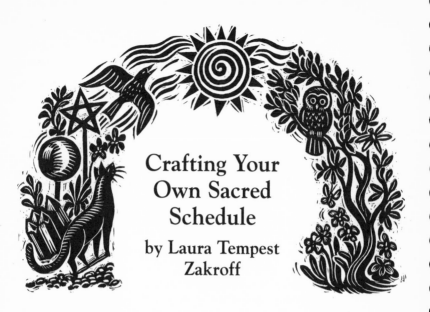

Crafting Your Own Sacred Schedule

by Laura Tempest Zakroff

What days of the year are the most important to you? Are you making a place for them in your practice, or are you bypassing them altogether? What makes your year go 'round? These are important points to consider when finding your life rhythm and setting a sacred schedule for your own Wheel of the Year.

All too frequently, new practitioners approach this path and feel they must absorb a whole new system as directed by a book. That includes celebrating the Wheel of the Year down to the letter, even if it doesn't make sense for your location, background, beliefs, myths, real life experiences, and so on. This approach can leave you feeling out of touch with what's happening around you or even make you wonder if you're doing your witchery all wrong.

But there are very few hard and fast rules in Witchcraft—instead, there are many suggestions and recommended guidelines. The Wheel of the Year model, as it appears in most books over the last fifty years, is a relatively new construction pieced together from different traditions. I'm not pointing this fact out to knock this system—it does work well for many people. Yet it can be all too easy to forget that the Wheel of the Year is a guideline, not a rule to be adhered to religiously or exclusively. The intention behind its formation is to give modern Pagans a cycle they can connect with. How you mark or celebrate the seasons, mythic changes, and important dates will depend heavily on the foundation of your personal practice.

Take into consideration that the popular version of Wheel of the Year is heavily steeped in Celtic myth. What if you wish to delve into your Slavic, Japanese, or Brazilian heritage? Every culture has its own vibrant collection of myths and sacred days. Sometimes they overlap with the eight sabbats, similarly landing on solstices, equinoxes, or the cross-quarter days, but sometimes they don't. For example, the Slavic/Russian

sun-oriented feast of Kupala occurs in early July while Obon, a Japanese festival that honors the dead, falls in mid-August.

There's also the problematic trappings of a culture that insists on separating the sacred from the secular. Big festivals and feast days help bring a community together, but that doesn't mean they are more special or powerful than days that have deep personal meaning in your own life. When we are able to see the correlations between the big moments and our day-to-day lives, we enhance our ability to connect with the world around us. The more we can honor and celebrate the seasons of our own lives, the deeper our practice becomes.

Anniversaries, Birthdays, and Other Important Life Moments

This first category may seem pretty obvious, but we often tend to not look at these dates in a spiritual context. We may even view them as obligations versus observances over time. Birthdays aren't just about getting older; they are opportunities to reflect on the events that took place in the past year and set goals for the next year. A birthday can serve as a reminder for us to be kinder to ourselves.

Marking the beginning of a relationship (wedding, union, handfasting, etc.) is a great time to remember what brought you together and what you have accomplished along the way. Similarly, anniversaries of endings can be moments to recall how far we've come and how we have changed. For example, nearly a decade after the fact, I still remember the date when I finally decided to end an abusive relationship. It marks not only that end but also a new beginning, the new me. Celebrate your moments of strength in dark times as well as your triumphs in the best of times.

What other important moments mark significant changes in your life? A college graduation date, the day you arrived in a new place, an initiation or elevation into a tradition, the day you met your best friend, or the day you reconciled with someone—all are possible things you might choose to acknowledge on a yearly basis.

Celebrating the Deceased

There is a tendency to think of the dead at certain times of the year, such as Samhain. But if you work with spirits and the deceased enough, you will find they are around us all year long. I celebrate my loved ones who have crossed over on their birthdays. Some people may choose to celebrate the deathday, but I prefer the birthday. Why? Well, on a technical level, I tend to only remember the season of someone's passing, not the actual date, so that's not really helpful. The main reason for using their date of birth, though, is that I want to celebrate their life and the impact they had on the world while they were alive.

Saint and Deity Days

While certain sabbats may have associations with specific deities, what if those gods aren't deities you feel connected to? Maybe the one or ones you choose to work with historically have a special date used to honor them. If you can't find a specific date or season in the records, you might use the day of dedication instead, if you have performed such a rite. Or you could use divination or trance work to determine which day would be pleasing to them.

There's also a fair amount of folks who have fondness for saints—whether because they are coming from a Catholic background or they made a connection to that saint via their current path. In some religions, the deities of old became saints because the powers that

be couldn't squash the belief in them, so they were "legitimatized" instead. In other instances, they can be viewed as the Mighty Dead, or enlightened humans who act as intermediaries to the divine.

Family and Familiar Feasts

Is there a particular occasion that has been long-celebrated in your family or has a special place in your heart? Carry on that tradition then! Even if it is tied to a religious tradition that you no longer follow or is completely secular in origin, consider what makes that day special to you. Is the meaning rooted in who was in attendance, the time of year, or what meal was always served? Think about what spiritual or magical context can that feast have for you now. Traditions survive through a healthy mixture of both preservation and change.

Local Festivities

Where we live has a huge impact on how we turn the Wheel. The landscape, the seasons, and the local culture all affect how we experience the world around us. The community in which you live probably already has festivals that honor certain changes, such as a harvest festival, an annual block party, a yearly parade to commemorate an event in the town's history, or a natural phenomenon that happens like clockwork (monsoons, fog season, second summer, etc). These modern-day observances can have just as much power as the commonly accepted sabbats—and even more personal meaning for you because the event directly reflects the spirit of where you live. Remember, everything has an origin!

Follow Your Roots

Not only is it important to acknowledge the patterns of the land where you live, but you may also find exploring your roots very inspiring. Where are your ancestors from? What traditions and celebrations did they observe historically? You probably won't find books on these subjects in the New Age section of the library or bookstore—instead you'll want to wander over to the anthropology and folklore sections. If a particular tradition or day really resonates with you, consider how you can sincerely explore it. Are the people who live in that area today still observing it? Can you find videos online of the festivities? It might be worth a trip to immerse yourself more and see what you can discover about your roots.

How Do You Celebrate?

Now, all this exploration doesn't mean that every day you note as important must be acknowledged with elaborate ritual. Lighting a candle on your altar, taking a few moments to meditate outside, or preparing the favorite meal of a deceased loved one all work beautifully. If you know a particular day is going to hit you hard emotionally or mentally, then remember to schedule in self-care of some kind. That care can be anything from taking a cleansing bath to scheduling an outing with friends to dedicating the day to doing community service.

Working with Hecate

by James Kambos

She has been feared and adored. She has been known by many names—the Nameless One, the One Who Stands Alone, and the Enchantress. In ancient poetry from Egypt, it seems she was even referred to as the Great Mother. She is a destroyer and, at the same time, a giver of life. To those who harm the innocent, her revenge can be swift and brutal; but to those who follow a path of righteousness, she is known as a protector.

She is Hecate, and she is one of the most ancient and complex goddesses the world has ever known. Her power is legendary. Zeus, the mightiest of the Greek gods, honored her and allowed her to grant, or withhold, wishes from humans—a power usually reserved for only Zeus himself.

The origins of Hecate as a goddess and where she was first worshipped remain as mysterious as the goddess herself. But one thing is certain: time has not diminished her charisma nor her power as a magician/Witch. For proof of this we only need to be reminded that Shakespeare, the greatest playwright in history, included Hecate in a pivotal role in one of the greatest plays of all time—*Macbeth*. In *Macbeth* it is Hecate's magic that leads to Macbeth's downfall.

It's no wonder that many Witches today wish to work with Hecate and want to make this fascinating goddess their personal deity. But how do you do that, and where do you start?

Well, it won't happen overnight. First, you'll need to learn some history and background about Hecate.

Hecate: An Ancient Goddess

Hecate is older than most of the deities known in ancient Greece. How old exactly, no one is certain. Some say her worship began in Asia Minor. My guess is that she may have had a following even earlier, in Egypt perhaps. In ancient Egypt there was a word—*hekau*. Its meaning is obscure. It may have meant "magic" or "amulet." It has also been suggested that there may have been a goddess named Hekau. The point is, the word *hekau* and the name *Hecate* are similar. It appears that hekau meant something referring to the magical arts in ancient Egypt. So I don't think it could be ruled out to say that Hecate may have originated in another culture, such as Egypt's, before being worshipped by the ancient Greeks. We may never know for sure.

We do know that Hecate is a triple goddess. But I don't mean in the Maiden-Mother-Crone concept commonly accepted by many modern Witches. Originally, Hecate was the triple goddess of the heavens, the earth, and the underworld. This is how she should still be honored today. She's also a Moon goddess, governing the waning and dark phases. Above all, Hecate is the supreme goddess of magic, Witchcraft, and spirits.

As a triple goddess, she was originally depicted with three heads and six arms, carrying daggers and torches. At her feet were serpents, and by her side were three dogs. Later she was frequently depicted as single-bodied with three faces. Sometimes she was accompanied by a three-headed dog at her side.

Hecate's Symbols and Signs

The symbols and signs associated with Hecate are many, and their meanings are rich and varied. It's said if you see any of these signs frequently or in an unusual manner, it's a signal that Hecate is reaching out to you. Pay attention—Hecate may already want to work with you. There may be more signs than what I mention here, but these are some of the more common ones.

Since Hecate is a triple goddess, let's take a look at numbers associated with her. Naturally, three is one of her numbers, but so are six and nine. Some also consider thirteen one of her numbers.

Keys are sacred to her. They symbolize her ability to lock up or release spirits, ghosts, or demons at her command. The key is also associated with Hecate's ability to unlock and enter the underworld.

Torches are also important to Hecate. Torches light her way to and from the underworld. She also uses them at night on earth as she wanders graveyards, leading souls to rest and to the underworld. We should also remember Hecate was the goddess who used her torch to help Demeter find her daughter, Persephone, after her abduction by Hades.

Animals linked to Hecate include horses, fish, dogs—especially black dogs—and black cats. Owls have a special meaning for her as well. Remember, owls are messengers from the other side (the underworld), one of her realms. Serpents are also associated with her.

Since Hecate is linked to the earth, she's long been associated with abundance. Her special food and herbs include barley, onion, garlic, fish, honey, cheese, and mugwort. Olive oil, water, and wine are favored by her also.

With her ability to pass at will between heaven, earth, and the underworld, it makes sense that Hecate is connected to physical boundaries such as doors, gates, walls, fences, and property lines or to any other portal or barrier. Since ancient times, her followers have gathered to leave offerings at one of her favorite places: crossroads, especially three-way intersections. Her comings and goings at these roadways were announced by the baying of dogs.

Hecate's colors are black, silver, white, and purple. Pearls and moonstones are her gems. Silver is her metal. The ritual tool most closely associated with her is probably the cauldron, since when it's empty, it's dark like the night sky, one of her realms.

You may know of or have used other symbols and tools to connect with Hecate. The ones I've mentioned have worked for me, and I hope they've given you some new ideas. What follows are some thoughts about working with Hecate as a personal deity.

Hecate as a Personal Deity

To dedicate yourself to Hecate and make her your personal deity is a big step in your spiritual growth. Read all you can about her. She is no-nonsense but fair. Many of her followers will tell you that she will let you know if she wants you to work with her by sending you some "signs." Let's look at what some of these signs could be.

First, be on the lookout for any of Hecate's animals wanting to be near you or wanting to help you. Is there suddenly a friendly stray dog or black cat in your neighborhood? Have you heard an owl hoot, and you've never heard one before? For me it was the day a black Labrador retriever helped me by chasing away a pesky little dog. I knew Hecate was watching out for me!

Or you may see many of her other symbols. For example, maybe you'll see a large collection of old keys in an antique shop. Then again, you may begin seeing her numbers—three, six, and nine—with greater frequency.

Pay attention to your dreams too. Do you see roads, dark alleys, or doors? These are some of her favored places. Dreaming of a deceased loved one could also be a sign from Hecate.

Next, set up an altar dedicated to her. Near your front door is a good place, or, since she likes seclusion, a corner, an alcove, and even a small closet are good choices. Cover the altar with black, gray, or purple fabric. Decorate it with statues or images of Hecate and her favorite animals. Include a black cauldron and black, silver, white, or purple candles. A key, especially if its origin is unknown, would be a nice touch.

After the altar is ready, leave Hecate an offering. Some dried barley, a piece of cake, or red wine are a few ideas. Try to honor her on the last day of the Dark Moon phase with an offering. If you honor Hecate only one time of the year, it should be the evening of November 16. This is the Night of Hecate, when her followers would leave offerings of food at a crossroads.

When you feel you've established a relationship with Hecate, then you may seek her help. She's the one to ask for help if your home needs protection. Also, seek her help in legal matters, if you've had something stolen, or in matters of property line boundaries.

After working with Hecate, you'll find her to be a goddess you can turn to in times of need. During rough times when you think you're alone, this ancient goddess—the One Who Stands Alone—will actually be hovering nearby when you need her the most.

January 2020

S	M	T	W
			1 New Year's Day
5	6	7	8
12	13	14	15
19	20 Martin Luther King Jr. Day Sun enters Aquarius	21	22
26	27	28	29
2	3	4	5

T	F	S	Notes
☾	3	4	
9	☺ Cold Moon Lunar Eclipse	11	
16	◖	18	
23	☽	25	
30	31	1	
6	7	8	

December/January

30 Monday

1st ≈
☽ v/c 5:24 am
☽ enters ♓ 10:41 am
Color: Ivory

Hanukkah ends

31 Tuesday

1st ♓
Color: White

New Year's Eve

1 Wednesday

1st ♓
☽ v/c 9:14 pm
☽ enters ♈ 11:00 pm
Color: Yellow

New Year's Day
Kwanzaa ends

◑ Thursday

1st ♈
2nd quarter 11:45 pm
Color: Turquoise

3 Friday

2nd ♈
♂ enters ♐ 4:37 am
☽ v/c 8:18 pm
Color: Pink

Set in Eastern Standard Time (EST)

Black Pepper Essential Oil

Black pepper essential oil is energizing, grounding, and protective. Inhaling the scent awakens the mind and fills us with an awareness of our own power and strength. If you need an extra dose of courage, take some deep breaths, open a bottle, and take a whiff. Feel the power of pepper filling your awareness and energy field, bolstering your confidence, and awakening your sense that—whatever it is—you can do it.

Psychic work can be enhanced by the scent of black pepper. Inhale it while centering yourself before divination or when looking deeply into a situation to gain intuitive insight. It has a unique ability to tether you to the physical realm while simultaneously stimulating your third eye and awakening your crystal clear inner knowing. And by bolstering physical energy, it can be helpful for psychics and intuitives who tend to feel drained while utilizing their gifts. Create a charm for focus and confidence (helpful for things like job interviews and test taking) by tying a hematite into muslin with red yarn. Anoint it with essential oil of pepper, and keep it with you as needed. Refresh the essential oil with each use.

—Tess Whitehurst

---

4 Saturday
2nd ♈
☽ enters ♉ 11:15 am
Color: Gray

For safe travel, carry chalcedony or orange zircon.

---

5 Sunday
2nd ♉
Color: Amber

January

6 Monday

2nd ♉
☽ v/c 7:08 am
☽ enters ♊ 9:11 pm
Color: Silver

Mosi-oa-Tunya (The Smoke That Thunders), or Victoria
Falls, in Zambia and Zimbabwe is sacred to local tribes.

7 Tuesday

2nd ♊
Color: White

Contentment and contemplation are strengths of the
iguana spirit animal, much needed in today's hectic world.

8 Wednesday

2nd ♊
☽ v/c 5:16 pm
Color: Brown

9 Thursday

2nd ♊
☽ enters ♋ 3:43 am
Color: Purple

☺ Friday

2nd ♋
Full Moon 2:21 pm
☽ v/c 6:58 pm
♅ D 8:49 pm
Color: Rose

Cold Moon
Lunar Eclipse 2:21 pm, 20° ♋ 00'

Full Moon in Cancer

The first Full Moon of the year co-incides with a lunar eclipse and is in its own sign, Cancer. Cancer is the embodiment of the sacred feminine, aligned with the tides of the ocean and the cycles of women's fertility. It connects with the archetype of the Great Mother, underlining themes of home, tribe, belonging, ancestral roots, sustenance, sanctuary, and the unspoken emotional connections to the people in our life. Cancer wisdom teaches us about the need for bound-aries as well as when it is time to retreat to take care of ourselves. When her daughter is kidnapped by Hades, Demeter retreats to the land of Eleusis. The shifting currents of this Full Moon may bring forgotten memories to the surface, not only our own, but whispers of ancestral memories passed down by the women who came before us. This is a good time to turn our attention to working with lineage, tradition, and the wisdom of the Grandmothers.

Great Mother, give me the wisdom to know when it is time to retreat and to nurture not only others but also myself.

Guiding Goddesses: Demeter, Danu, Isis, Parvati

—Danielle Blackwood

---

11 Saturday

3rd ♋
☽ enters ♌ 7:16 am
Color: Blue

---

12 Sunday

3rd ♌
Color: Orange

Cypress brings clarity and emotional healing.

January

13 Monday

3rd ♌
☽ v/c 8:42 am
☽ enters ♍ 9:06 am
♀ enters ♓ 1:39 pm
Color: White

14 Tuesday

3rd ♍
Color: Black

Tarragon improves compassion and aids in healing from abuse.

15 Wednesday

3rd ♍
☽ v/c 7:12 am
☽ enters ♎ 10:43 am
Color: Yellow

16 Thursday

3rd ♎
☿ enters ♒ 1:31 pm
Color: Crimson

*Spicy and redolent, frankincense purifies and
protects. Add it to incense blends to boost their power.*

☽ Friday

3rd ♎
☽ v/c 7:58 am
4th quarter 7:58 am
☽ enters ♏ 1:20 pm
Color: Purple

Set in Eastern Standard Time (EST)

18 Saturday
4th ♏
Color: Black

19 Sunday
4th ♏
☽ v/c 4:22 pm
☽ enters ♐ 5:41 pm
Color: Gold

A tabard is a long rectangle of cloth with a head hole in the middle; throw it over regular clothes to indicate ritual roles.

20 Monday
4th ♐
☉ enters ≈ 9:55 am
☽ v/c 11:46 pm
Color: Ivory

Martin Luther King Jr. Day
Sun enters Aquarius

21 Tuesday
4th ♐
Color: Maroon

Celtic Tree Month of Rowan begins

22 Wednesday
4th ♈
☽ enters ♈ 12:00 am
Color: Topaz

23 Thursday
4th ♈
☽ v/c 9:08 pm
Color: Green

If the candle won't extinguish, it means you're not done
working; sit down and think about whether you missed a step.

☽ Friday
4th ♈
☽ enters ≈ 8:20 am
New Moon 4:42 pm
Color: Coral

Cheese Straws

1 cup all-purpose flour
½ tsp. baking powder
½ tsp. English mustard powder
   (or ½ tsp. cayenne pepper)
Pinch salt
¼ cup butter
½ cup strong cheese, grated
1 large egg yolk, beaten
2–4 tsp. milk

Sift the flour, baking powder, salt, and mustard into a bowl, and rub in the butter with your fingertips. Add the cheese, egg yolk, and enough milk to make a stiff dough. Roll out to about ⅛ inch thick and cut into "straws" about 2½ inches long and ¼ inch wide. Bake at 400°F for 10–15 minutes or until pale gold—do not be tempted to overcook. Cool on a wire rack.

At Imbolc we feel the very first stirrings of spring, and this is the time of first lambing; one of the translations of *Imbolc* is "ewe's milk," demonstrating that birth and nurturing exists even in the depths of winter. It is a promise of what is to come, and as a token it is traditional to include dairy produce in the seasonal feast.

—Anna Franklin

---

25 Saturday

1st ≈
☽ v/c 2:06 pm
Color: Gray

Lunar New Year (Rat)

---

26 Sunday

1st ≈
☽ enters ♓ 6:44 pm
Color: Yellow

January/February

27 Monday

1st ♓︎
Color: Lavender

28 Tuesday

1st ♓︎
☽ v/c 8:08 pm
Color: Scarlet

*Samantabhadri is the primordial mother
goddess in Tibet. She stands for absolute truth.*

29 Wednesday

1st ♓︎
☽ enters ♈︎ 6:51 am
Color: White

*White brings blessings and forgiveness. It
can erase mistakes with white-hot power.*

30 Thursday

1st ♈︎
Color: Purple

31 Friday

1st ♈︎
☽ v/c 10:10 am
☽ enters ♉︎ 7:28 pm
Color: Rose

Set in Eastern Standard Time (EST)

Imbolc and the Star

At Imbolc we help turn the Wheel of the Year by calling to the Goddess, asking her to return from the underworld. We make the world ready for her return, encouraged by the gentle signs of spring. The Star tarot card resonates with Imbolc's themes of grace, spiritual nourishment, purification, healing, hope, peace, and gentleness. While Yule, when the darkness still holds sway, requires faith, Imbolc, like the Star, grants grace. We now see that the light is returning, and we can rest in that certainty. Like the ewe's milk for which this holiday is named, the Star promises nourishment for body and soul. Symbols in the Star include water, a sign of cleansing, healing, and renewal. In the same way that mothers prepare for birth with clarity of purpose, use the Star to focus on your own personal North Star, a light that clearly guides you on your path. Filled with grace and purified by inner healing, find the strength and motivation to give birth to the best within you as well as prepare the way for Great Mother's return.

—Barbara Moore

◑ Saturday

1st ♉
2nd quarter 8:42 pm
Color: Indigo

> *"Water gives life to the ten thousand things and does not strive. It flows in places men reject and so is like the Tao."* —Tao Te Ching

2 Sunday

2nd ♉
Color: Gold

Imbolc
Groundhog Day

February 2020

S	M	T	W
2 Imbolc Groundhog Day	3	4	5
☺ Quickening Moon	10	11	12
16 Mercury Retrograde	17 Presidents' Day	18 Sun enters Pisces	19
☽ 	24	25	26
1	2	3	4

T	F	S	Notes
		☾	
6	7	8	
13	14	☽	
	Valentine's Day		
20	21	22	
27	28	29	
5	6	7	

February

3 Monday
2nd ♉
☽ v/c 6:28 am
☽ enters ♊ 6:29 am
☿ enters ♓ 6:37 am
Color: Gray

Bamapana is a trickster god from Australia.
Invoke him for inspiration in rude language.

4 Tuesday
2nd ♊
Color: Red

Imbolc crossquarter day (Sun reaches 15° Aquarius)

5 Wednesday
2nd ♊
☽ v/c 9:20 am
☽ enters ♋ 2:03 pm
Color: White

6 Thursday

2nd ♋
Color: Green

Green relates to hope and promise. It
works especially well for money magic.

7 Friday

2nd ♋
☽ v/c 10:43 am
♀ enters ♈ 3:02 pm
☽ enters ♌ 5:45 pm
Color: Purple

Full Moon in Leo

The Full Moon in Leo is connected to the archetypes of the Queen, the King, and the Divine Child. It is a time to embrace our personal sovereignty and to stand fully in our power. Sovereignty is about showing up with authenticity. Having agency over our bodies, sexuality, and life choices. Taking back power that has been given away or stolen. Saying no to the need for approval or for permission to be yourself. The Welsh sovereignty goddess Rhiannon teaches us to speak

from our heart and to walk with dignity and generosity of spirit no matter what challenges life brings. The Leo Full Moon also underlines the themes of creative self-expression as well as owning and celebrating our unique ways of being in the world. This Full Moon is a time to allow your creativity free reign and to bring a dream or idea to fruition. It is a time to celebrate, to cultivate confidence, and make space for pleasure.

Rhiannon, show me how to hold my head high and know that I am the sovereign queen of my own life.

Guiding Goddesses: Rhiannon, Macha, Maeve

—Danielle Blackwood

---

8 Saturday

2nd ♌
Color: Blue

☺ Sunday

2nd ♌
Full Moon 2:33 am
☽ v/c 11:08 am
☽ enters ♍ 6:39 pm
Color: Amber

Quickening Moon

February

10 Monday
3rd ♍
Color: Ivory

11 Tuesday
3rd ♍
☽ v/c 1:26 pm
☽ enters ♎ 6:37 pm
Color: Scarlet

To remove hexes, rub the body with a slice
of yucca root every day for seven days.

12 Wednesday
3rd ♎
Color: Brown

Kishijoten is the Japanese goddess of luck and
beauty. She lends her grace to the geishas.

13 Thursday
☽ v/c 4:40 pm
☽ enters ♏ 7:37 pm
Color: Turquoise

14 Friday
3rd ♏
Color: Coral

Valentine's Day

Set in Eastern Standard Time (EST)

Neroli Essential Oil

With a sweet, white floral scent, the citrus blossom from which neroli essential oil is derived is simultaneously delicate and hearty, earthy and otherworldly. Among the most romantic of scents, neroli opens the heart, awakens the senses, invites lasting love, and encourages harmonious commitment. It also relieves stress, relaxes the body, and promotes restful sleep. Inhale the scent to relieve and restructure negative, harsh, or self-limiting thought patterns and to enhance feelings of euphoria and joy. Diffuse the scent in a space to heal challenging relationship patterns and create a peaceful environment. Diffuse it during spells or rituals for domestic bliss, marital harmony, and a happy home. Wear neroli (in a carrier oil or in a blend) to attract a long-term romantic partner. To perform a simple candle spell for the same purpose, anoint a white candle with sweet almond oil containing neroli, and light it on a Friday during a waxing Moon. If you feel depressed, stuck, anxious, or ungrounded, add 8 to 10 drops to your bathwater and soak for 20 to 40 minutes to open your heart and rediscover your inner equilibrium. Carry a bottle and inhale as needed.

—Tess Whitehurst

☾ Saturday

3rd ♏
4th quarter 5:17 pm
☾ v/c 5:20 pm
☾ enters ♐ 11:07 pm
Color: Gray

Hummingbirds convey speed and a connection with the numinous; they literally live on a faster plane of existence.

---

16 Sunday

4th ♐
♂ enters ♑ 6:33 am
☿ ℞ 7:54 pm
Color: Orange

Mercury retrograde until March 9

February

17 Monday
4th ♐
Color: White

Presidents' Day

18 Tuesday
4th ♐
☽ v/c 4:03 am
☽ enters ♑ 5:37 am
☉ enters ♓ 11:57 pm
Color: Black

Celtic Tree Month of Ash begins
Sun enters Pisces

19 Wednesday
4th ♑
Color: Yellow

20 Thursday
4th ♑
☽ v/c 9:18 am
☽ enters ♒ 2:42 pm
Color: Purple

To attract friendship use chrysoprase,
pink tourmaline, and turquoise.

21 Friday
4th ♒
☽ v/c 11:08 pm
Color: Pink

22 Saturday

4th ≈
Color: Black

☽ Sunday

4th ≈
☽ enters ♓ 1:37 am
New Moon 10:32 am
Color: Yellow

*Linden is generally soothing, with the
ability to relieve stress and bring sleep.*

February/March

24 Monday
1st ♓
Color: Silver

25 Tuesday
1st ♓
☽ v/c 9:12 am
☽ enters ♈ 1:47 pm
Color: Maroon

Mardi Gras (Fat Tuesday)

26 Wednesday
1st ♈
Color: Topaz

Ash Wednesday

27 Thursday
1st ♈
☽ v/c 10:25 pm
Color: White

28 Friday
1st ♈
☽ enters ♉ 2:30 am
Color: Rose

When wax drips on only one side of a
candle, it indicates something out of balance.

Set in Eastern Standard Time (EST)

Spearmint Essential Oil

Sweeter, smoother, and less piquant than peppermint (but no less powerful), spearmint essential oil is instantly calming and uplifting. While peppermint provides a cool, bracing jolt, spearmint provides a soothing awakening to the senses and present moment. Simultaneously, its relaxing properties support stress relief and restful sleep.

An excellent energy cleanser, spearmint essential oil can be added to spring water to create a delightful smudge spray. Place 10 to 20 drops in a bucket of warm water to make a great space-clearing floor wash. Use the same formula to wash your front door to invite in an abundance of blessings and wealth.

Diffuse spearmint oil during magic related to all forms of healing; it is a wonderful way to support emotional healing, heart healing, and healing from any type of trauma. Empaths and other sensitive folk will find it helpful to carry a bottle and inhale the scent regularly for energetic protection and to restructure and repair the auric field. As you inhale, imagine your body being filled and surrounded with a protective mint-green light.

—Tess Whitehurst

---

29 Saturday
1st ♉
Color: Brown

Priestesses may wear a circlet with a
crescent Moon or Moon phases, usually silver.

---

1 Sunday
1st ♉
☽ v/c 10:52 am
☽ enters ♊ 2:21 pm
Color: Yellow

March 2020

S	M	T	W
1	●	3	4
8 Daylight Saving Time begins at 2 am	☻ Storm Moon Mercury Direct	10	11
15	◖	17 St. Patrick's Day	18
22	23	☽	25
29	30	31	1
5	6	7	8

T	F	S	Notes
5	6	7	
12	13	14	
19	20	21	
Ostara / Spring Equinox Sun enters Aries			
26	27	28	
2	3	4	
9	10	11	

March

O Monday

1st ♊
2nd quarter 2:57 pm
Color: Ivory

3 Tuesday

2nd ♊
☽ v/c 9:20 pm
☽ enters ♋ 11:25 pm
Color: Black

*Patchouli is dark and earthy. Burn it for
prosperity, security, and earth magic.*

4 Wednesday

2nd ♋
☿ enters ≈ 6:08 am
♀ enters ♉ 10:07 pm
Color: Brown

5 Thursday

2nd ♋
Color: Purple

*Eototo is a Native American weather
god. He controls the wind and clouds.*

6 Friday

2nd ♋
☽ v/c 2:11 am
☽ enters ♌ 4:27 am
Color: White

7 Saturday

2nd ♌
Color: Black

The Mahabodhi Tree in India marks
where the Buddha attained enlightenment.

8 Sunday

2nd ♌
☽ v/c 4:12 am
☽ enters ♍ 6:47 am
Color: Amber

Daylight Saving Time begins at 2 am

March

☺ Monday

2nd ♍
Full Moon 1:48 pm
☿ D 11:49 pm
Color: Lavender

Storm Moon

10 Tuesday

3rd ♍
☽ v/c 4:32 am
☽ enters ♎ 6:03 am
Color: Red

Purim (begins at sundown on March 9)

11 Wednesday

3rd ♎
Color: Yellow

Glastonbury Tor in England is sacred to the Goddess.

12 Thursday

3rd ♎
☽ v/c 4:12 am
☽ enters ♏ 5:28 am
Color: White

Good healing stones include agate, garnet, and jade.

13 Friday

3rd ♏
Color: Rose

Set in Eastern Daylight Time (EDT)

Full Moon in Virgo

During the Full Moon in Virgo, we turn to the task of separating the grain from the chaff, to bring the things of our lives to order. Virgo is the practical priestess—the Healer—connected to the archetype of the Virgin Goddess, Hestia, who teaches us the value of intentional solitude. Virgo medicine shows us how to be discriminating and hone things down to their essentials. She is the solitary Witch in the forest who tends herbs by the Moon. The

one who knows that the rituals of daily life are sacred, that the body is the temple, and that service is a spiritual practice. Now is the time to synthesize, refine, and make the things of our lives sound. To know just what medicine is required, to dispel illusion and see into the heart of the matter.

Hestia, help me sort the seeds. Help me know when it is time to harvest and when it is time to let something die on the vine. Show me the magic of a simple, well-ordered life.

Guiding Goddesses: Hestia, Astraea, Frigg

—Danielle Blackwood

---

14 Saturday

3rd ♏︎
☽ v/c 6:06 am
☽ enters ♐︎ 7:09 am
Color: Blue

Blue is soothing and cleansing. Use it for water magic.

---

15 Sunday

3rd ♐︎
Color: Orange

March

○ Monday
3rd ♐
☿ enters ♓ 3:42 am
☽ v/c 5:34 am
4th quarter 5:34 am
☽ enters ♑ 12:25 pm
Color: Gray

17 Tuesday
4th ♑
Color: Maroon

St. Patrick's Day

18 Wednesday
4th ♑
☽ v/c 8:48 pm
☽ enters ♒ 9:16 pm
Color: Topaz

Celtic Tree Month of Alder begins

19 Thursday
4th ♒
☉ enters ♈ 11:50 pm
Color: Green

Ostara/Spring Equinox
International Astrology Day
Sun enters Aries

20 Friday
4th ♒
☽ v/c 5:00 am
Color: Purple

Ostara and Temperance

At Ostara, the Goddess returns from the underworld, bringing with her a celebration of miracles, spring, new life, and balance. The Temperance tarot card beautifully represents these themes. Birth is considered a kind of miracle, a mixing of life and death (for the minute anything is born, it begins to die) that creates our experience on this planet. The angel in Temperance holds two cups, their liquid blending at a scientifically impossible angle, representing an alchemical mystery.

Although equinoxes represent balance, and at this time life and light are becoming stronger than death and darkness, each equinox contains the seed of its opposite. Like an eggshell—which is strong enough to protect new life but at the right moment is weak enough to be broken through— something is destroyed and the old existence of the newly born creature dies. Temperance is often shown with a Sun disk on the angel's head, a glowing yellow crown in the distance, and yellow daffodils at the angel's feet. Work with these symbols to explore the power and necessity of the Sun in your physical and spiritual life.

—Barbara Moore

21 Saturday

4th ♒
☽ enters ♓ 8:33 am
♄ enters ♒ 11:58 pm
Color: Indigo

A cord typically measures the wearer's height and may be worn around the waist of a robe or other garment.

22 Sunday

4th ♓
Color: Gold

March

23 Monday

4th ♓
☽ v/c 10:51 am
☽ enters ♈ 8:58 pm
Color: Silver

☽ Tuesday

4th ♈
New Moon 5:28 am
Color: Gray

The seahorse represents the masculine ability to
nurture a family, a great spirit animal for househusbands.

25 Wednesday

1st ♈
Color: White

26 Thursday

1st ♈
☽ v/c 3:16 am
☽ enters ♉ 9:37 am
Color: Turquoise

27 Friday

1st ♉
Color: Coral

To bring luck carry apache tear, cross stone, or jet.

Set in Eastern Daylight Time (EDT)

Anglesey Eggs

Eggs are a symbol of renewal at this season, as it was the time when birds began to lay, which is why we have eggs at Easter!

6 leeks, sliced
1½ cups cooked potato, mashed
Salt and pepper
2 T. butter
3 T. all-purpose flour
1¼ cups milk
⅔ cup grated cheese
8 hard-boiled eggs, sliced

Boil the leeks in salted water for 10 minutes. Strain well and mix with the mashed potato. Season, add half the butter, and beat together. Pack this mixture around the edge and bottom of a pie dish to form a pie "crust." Melt the rest of the butter in a pan and stir in the flour. Gradually add the milk, whisking continually to make a sauce. When it has thickened, remove from heat and add the cheese, reserving a little to sprinkle on top. Put the hard-boiled eggs into the center of your pie and cover with the cheese sauce. Sprinkle the rest of the cheese on top and bake at 400°F until golden brown.

—Anna Franklin

---

28 Saturday

1st ☿
☽ v/c 7:05 pm
☽ enters ♊ 9:38 pm
Color: Gray

In Africa, Yasigi is the goddess of alcohol and dancing. Her icons appear with big breasts and masks.

---

29 Sunday

1st ♊
Color: Amber

April 2020

S	M	T	W
			☾ All Fools' Day
5	6	☺ Wind Moon	8
12	13	☾	15
19 Sun enters Taurus	20	21	☽ Earth Day
26	27	28	29
3	4	5	6

T	F	S	Notes
2	3	4	
9	10	11	
16	17	18	
23	24	25	
◖	1	2	
7	8	9	

30 Monday
1st ♊
☽ v/c 11:10 am
♂ enters ♒ 3:43 pm
Color: White

*A small but steady candle flame
means low, diffuse energy in a spell.*

31 Tuesday
1st ♊
☽ enters ♋ 7:43 am
Color: Scarlet

◐ Wednesday
1st ♋
2nd quarter 6:21 am
Color: Topaz

All Fools' Day
April Fools' Day

2 Thursday
2nd ♋
☽ v/c 12:49 pm
☽ enters ♌ 2:26 pm
Color: Green

3 Friday
2nd ♌
♀ enters ♊ 1:11 pm
☽ v/c 3:29 pm
Color: Pink

If seeking peace, keep aquamarine, malachite, or sapphire.

Chamomile Essential Oil

Among the most soothing of essential oils is chamomile. With a scent reminiscent of baking bread, bananas, and the earth after it rains, chamomile smoothes the harsh edges of life, comforts the skin, relieves headaches, and supports restful sleep. Diffuse the essential oil during rituals designed to promote relaxation, peace, and calm. Carry a bottle with you and inhale throughout the day as an instant stress eraser. Inhale straight from the bottle or diffuse the scent to alleviate digestive upsets and chronic pain. Add it to body lotion and massage into the body to soothe irritated skin, promote sleep, and alleviate symptoms of menopause and PMS.

To heal blocks in the solar plexus chakra, add a few drops of chamomile to sunflower oil and anoint your upper stomach (solar plexus area) with the mixture. Create a smudge spray with equal parts essential oil of chamomile, spearmint, and lavender in spring water to clear the space after an argument, calm angry vibrations, or facilitate mutually respectful interactions. The same formula is great for kids' rooms to help them wind down before bed.

—Tess Whitehurst

---

4 Saturday

2nd ♌
☽ enters ♍ 5:18 pm
Color: Blue

Stuff a dream pillow with valerian for peaceful sleep.

---

5 Sunday

2nd ♍
Color: Yellow

Palm Sunday

April

6 Monday
2nd ♍
☽ v/c 9:29 am
☽ enters ♎ 5:16 pm
Color: Gray

"There isn't shame in having shadows—we all have them to varying degrees. It's simply a part of being human."—Timothy Roderick

☺ Tuesday
2nd ♎
Full Moon 10:35 pm
Color: White

Wind Moon

8 Wednesday
3rd ♎
☽ v/c 8:50 am
☽ enters ♏ 4:17 pm
Color: Brown

9 Thursday
3rd ♏
Color: Crimson

Passover begins (at sundown on April 8)

10 Friday
3rd ♏
☽ v/c 3:35 pm
☽ enters ♐ 4:35 pm
Color: Rose

Good Friday

Set in Eastern Daylight Time (EDT)

Full Moon in Libra

The Libra Full Moon underlines the connection between Self and Other. Aligned with the goddess Venus and Aphrodite Urania, Libra is concerned with the art of relationship—not just of the romantic sort, but between all things. Themes of beauty, balance, fairness, and refined aesthetic come to the fore when the Moon is full in Libra. It is a good time for love magic: getting clear about defining your own needs in a relationship while artfully balancing the needs of others, working magic for deepening an existing union, and drawing the perfect person for you into your life (without naming names) are especially potent right now. Personal adornment is a sacred ritual to Libra, and this Full Moon highlights how we choose to show up in the world and put our best foot forward.

Aphrodite Urania, teach me the subtle arts of beauty, balance, and right relationship. Help me to remember that self-love is just as necessary as loving another. Remind me that all forms of beauty are a sacrament of the Goddess.

Guiding Goddesses: Aphrodite Urania, Lakshmi, Venus

—Danielle Blackwood

---

11 Saturday

3rd ♐
☿ enters ♈ 12:48 am
Color: Indigo

Akka is the Finnish earth goddess.
Call on her for feminine strength.

---

12 Sunday

3rd ♐
☽ v/c 7:46 am
☽ enters ♑ 8:05 pm
Color: Gold

Easter

April

13 Monday
3rd ♑
Color: Ivory

Amida is the Japanese god of light.
Turn to him for enlightenment.

○ Tuesday
3rd ♑
4th quarter 6:56 pm
☽ v/c 7:47 pm
Color: Red

Red is for fire and passion. It also means
"stop," making it ideal for blocking spells.

15 Wednesday
4th ♑
☽ enters ♒ 3:37 am
Color: Yellow

Celtic Tree Month of Willow begins

16 Thursday
4th ♒
Color: Turquoise

Passover ends

17 Friday
4th ♒
☽ v/c 10:34 am
☽ enters ♓ 2:29 pm
Color: Coral

Orthodox Good Friday

Set in Eastern Daylight Time (EDT)

18 Saturday

4th ♓
Color: Brown

19 Sunday

4th ♓
☉ enters ♉ 10:45 am
☽ v/c 7:31 pm
Color: Amber

Orthodox Easter
Sun enters Taurus

April

20 Monday
4th ♓
☽ enters ♈ 3:00 am
Color: Gray

*Orange tree balances masculine and
feminine energies, so it promotes partnership.*

21 Tuesday
4th ♈
Color: Black

☽ Wednesday
4th ♈
☽ v/c 8:32 am
☽ enters ♉ 3:36 pm
New Moon 10:26 pm
Color: White

Earth Day

23 Thursday
1st ♉
Color: Green

Ramadan begins

24 Friday
1st ♉
☽ v/c 8:43 pm
Color: Purple

*Dragon's blood is earthy, spicy, and a little sweet.
Burn it for oath-taking, abundance, or protection.*

Ylang-ylang Essential Oil

Ylang-ylang blossoms drip from their branches, fluttering in the island breeze. This essential oil's unique floral scent brings us into our senses and facilitates romance, relaxation, self-approval, and self-love. It's also a wonderful ally when healing from heartbreak, grief, trauma, or abuse.

In the Victorian era, ylang-ylang was added to scalp tonics to promote hair growth. For this purpose, try adding 10 drops to a bottle of shampoo. Shake well and wash with it daily, massaging it thoroughly into your scalp. Add 6 to 8 drops of ylang-ylang oil to a mister of rose water, shake, and mist your bedding to encourage relaxed intimacy. (Add a few drops of sandalwood for extra sweetness and attraction.) Or mist yourself to open your eyes to your own beauty. You can also mist any space to promote feelings of relaxation and calm. If you're prone to panic attacks or anxiety, carry a bottle with you and inhale the scent when you want to center and settle your mind and emotions. If you have trouble sleeping due to anxious or repetitive thought patterns, try diffusing ylang-ylang oil in your bedroom before you sleep.

—Tess Whitehurst

25 Saturday

1st ♉
☽ enters ♊ 3:20 am
♀ ℞ 2:54 pm
Color: Black

To help with sleep, put a moonstone
or blue tourmaline under your pillow.

26 Sunday

1st ♊
Color: Yellow

May 2020

S	M	T	W
3	4	5	6
10 Mother's Day	11	12	13
17	18	19	20 Sun enters Gemini
24	25 Memorial Day	26	27
31	1	2	3

T	F	S	Notes
	1	2	
	Beltane		
☺	8	9	
Flower Moon			
◖	15	16	
21	☽	23	
28	◗	30	
4	5	6	

April/May

27 Monday

1st ♊
☽ v/c 1:00 pm
☽ enters ♋ 1:28 pm
☿ enters ♉ 3:53 pm
Color: Silver

28 Tuesday

1st ♋
Color: Scarlet

Debris in a candle's melted wax means unintended
consequences of a spell; watch for things you need to clean up.

29 Wednesday

1st ♋
☽ v/c 3:29 pm
☽ enters ♌ 9:06 pm
Color: Brown

◖ Thursday

1st ♌
2nd quarter 4:38 pm
Color: Purple

Mythic spirit animals such as the unicorn or the dragon deal
extensively in magic and draw their power from collective attention.

1 Friday

2nd ♌
☽ v/c 12:04 pm
Color: Rose

Beltane/May Day

Set in Eastern Daylight Time (EDT)

Beltane and the Lovers

Beltane is a celebration of union and fertility, a symbolic wedding of the God and Goddess. During this holiday, we celebrate the things that delight our hearts as well as our bodies. We do things for the joy of them and not out of obligation or any other unhealthy reasons. The Divine Masculine and Divine Feminine join to create the Great Divine. In the Lovers card, some see a man and woman's union blessed by a higher being. Another

way to see it is that their union creates the presence of the Divine. While the Lovers card does suggest passion, sex, and romance, it is, at its root, about the joy and beauty of choosing wisely. In particular, it represents the act of choosing that which most satisfies the heart. Connect with this card to remember that it isn't that the Divine has a "plan" for you but that you, through your choices, help create how the Divine is expressed in the physical world. When we realize that, we realize that we have so much power and, consequently, so much responsibility.

—Barbara Moore

2 Saturday
2nd ♌
☽ enters ♍ 1:35 am
Color: Brown

3 Sunday
2nd ♍
☽ v/c 10:25 pm
Color: Gold

Callanish in Scotland is a stone circle around a burial chamber, with four avenues of smaller stones.

May

4 Monday

2nd ♍
☽ enters ♎ 3:09 am
Color: Ivory

Beltane crossquarter day (Sun reaches 15° Taurus)

5 Tuesday

2nd ♎
☽ v/c 10:31 pm
Color: Red

Cinco de Mayo

6 Wednesday

2nd ♎
☽ enters ♏ 3:05 am
Color: Topaz

"It is only with the heart that one can see rightly; what is essential is invisible to the eye." —Antoine de Saint-Exupery

☺ Thursday

2nd ♏
Full Moon 6:45 am
☽ v/c 10:39 pm
Color: Green

Flower Moon

8 Friday

3rd ♏
☽ enters ♐ 3:15 am
Color: White

Set in Eastern Daylight Time (EDT)

Full Moon in Scorpio

The Full Moon in Scorpio resonates with the mysteries of sex, birth, death, and rebirth. On this Full Moon we shine a light into the hidden recesses of our psyche. It is a time to shed old skins and let go of whatever is keeping us from growing. Under the Scorpio Full Moon, we have the opportunity for profound personal transformation. This is also a good time to reflect on how we can reclaim our sense of personal power. This Full Moon is an especially potent time to work with goddesses associated with the sacred dark. It is also time for working all kinds of banishing, releasing, and cord-cutting rituals. Scorpio helps us surrender to the process of transformation. Scorpio has a fierce compassion that tempers us, deepens us and turns us into beings of wisdom.

Inanna, walk beside me in my times of descent, and help me see that they are the pathways to wholeness, healing, and hard-won wisdom.

Guiding Goddesses: Inanna, the Morrigan, Kali, Cerridwen

—Danielle Blackwood

---

9 Saturday

3rd ♐
Color: Blue

---

10 Sunday

3rd ♐
☽ v/c 2:11 am
☽ enters ♑ 5:39 am
♄ ℞ 9:09 pm
Color: Orange

Mother's Day

May

11 Monday

3rd ♑
♄ ℞ 12:09 am
☿ enters ♊ 5:58 pm
Color: Lavender

As a spirit animal, the salamander features transformation and adaptability,
useful traits in a highly mobile society where people often change jobs.

12 Tuesday

3rd ♑
☽ v/c 6:30 am
☽ enters ♒ 11:39 am
Color: White

13 Wednesday

3rd ♒
♂ enters ♓ 12:17 am
♀ ℞ 2:45 am
Color: Yellow

Venus retrograde until June 25
Celtic Tree Month of Hawthorn begins

◯ Thursday

3rd ♒
☽ v/c 10:03 am
4th quarter 10:03 am
♃ ℞ 10:32 am
☽ enters ♓ 9:24 pm
Color: Turquoise

15 Friday

4th ♓
Color: Pink

Honey Custard

Beltane marks the return of summer and the flowering of the earth. This recipe makes use of honey, widely believed to be an aphrodisiac in ancient times, which gives us our word *honeymoon*, once thought to come from the period during which the bride and groom kept their own company and drank honey wine for a full month—or Moon—after the wedding.

2½ cups milk
2 T. honey
3 eggs
Pinch of salt

Put the milk in a pan and bring to nearly boiling. Stir in the honey. Remove from heat. In a large heatproof bowl, beat the eggs with the salt and then pour in the warm milk, stirring continually until blended. Pour into small ramekins and put these in a shallow pan. Carefully add boiling water to the pan so the water comes about halfway up the sides of the ramekins. Bake in the oven at 325°F for 40 minutes or until set. Allow to cool completely before serving.

—Anna Franklin

---

16 Saturday
4th ♓
Color: Gray

*Keep a fern in the room where you
study to improve mental function.*

---

17 Sunday
4th ♓
☽ v/c 3:59 am
☽ enters ♈ 9:36 am
Color: Yellow

*Yellow conjures happiness and uplifts the spirit.
This is why lemon is a fresh, cheerful scent.*

May

18 Monday
4th ♈
Color: Gray

Victoria Day (Canada)

19 Tuesday
4th ♈
☽ v/c 4:33 pm
☽ enters ♉ 10:10 pm
Color: Black

20 Wednesday
4th ♉
☉ enters ♊ 9:49 am
Color: White

Sun enters Gemini

21 Thursday
4th ♉
Color: Crimson

☽ Friday
4th ♉
☽ v/c 4:01 am
☽ enters ♊ 9:36 am
New Moon 1:39 pm
Color: Rose

A stole is a strip of material decorated with
holy symbols, usually worn by clergy.

Set in Eastern Daylight Time (EDT)

23 Saturday

1st ♊
Color: Blue

Ramadan ends

24 Sunday

1st ♊
☽ v/c 7:09 am
☽ enters ♋ 7:09 pm
Color: Amber

*Zakar is the Mesopotamian god of dreams and
esoteric messages. He can help make sense of symbolism.*

May

25 Monday
1st ♋
Color: Silver

Memorial Day

26 Tuesday
1st ♋
☽ v/c 9:06 pm
Color: Scarlet

27 Wednesday
1st ♋
☽ enters ♌ 2:33 am
Color: Brown

*Carved peach pits may be carried to drive
away evil, attract love, or promote fertility.*

28 Thursday
1st ♌
☽ v/c 9:30 am
☿ enters ♋ 2:09 pm
Color: White

☽ Friday
1st ♌
☽ enters ♍ 7:40 am
2nd quarter 11:30 pm
Color: Purple

Shavuot (begins at sundown on May 28)

Set in Eastern Daylight Time (EDT)

Tangerine Essential Oil

Tangerine is relaxing, energizing, inspiring, and sweet. Inhaling it is like a ray of sunshine after a storm. It brings balance to the digestion and can help alleviate anxiety, depression, insomnia, and symptoms of PMS. Magically, essential oil of tangerine magnetizes success. Diffuse it in your business or workspace to facilitate victory, accomplishment, and abundance. Create a wealth- and success-drawing charm by placing a citrine quartz point on a tiny dish of rolled oats. Dispense a few drops of tangerine essential oil onto the oats, and place it near your cash register, on your desk, or adjacent to your front door.

Add 10 to 12 drops of tangerine essential oil to a mister of spring water for a smudge spray to enhance feelings of positivity and harmony within a space. Add some lemon essential oil if you'd like it to double as an energizer and vibrational cleanser, or add some neroli if you'd like to swirl in some heart-opening vibes. Tangerine is also an excellent sleep ally: diffuse it in your bedroom before bedtime to promote sweet dreams and restful sleep.

—Tess Whitehurst

30 Saturday
2nd ♍
Color: Black

Black is mysterious and absorbing. It makes a trap for unwanted energies.

31 Sunday
2nd ♍
☽ v/c 5:17 am
☽ enters ♎ 10:38 am
Color: Orange

Prehistoric spirit animals such as the woolly mammoth or the triceratops are good for working with ancestors and deep history.

June 2020

S	M	T	W
	1	2	3
7	8	9	10
14 Flag Day	15	16	17
🌙 Father's Day Solar Eclipse	22	23	24
◐	29	30	1
5	6	7	8

	T	F	S	
	4	☻	6	**Notes**
		Strong Sun Moon Lunar Eclipse		
	11	12	◖	
	18	19	20	
	Mercury Retrograde		Litha / Summer Solstice Sun enters Cancer	
	25	26	27	
	2	3	4	
	9	10	11	

June

1 Monday
2nd ♎︎
Color: Lavender

*Alpan is the Etruscan goddess of love. She
wears nothing but her wings and sandals.*

2 Tuesday
2nd ♎︎
☽ v/c 6:40 am
☽ enters ♏︎ 12:06 pm
Color: Red

Hornbeam supports enthusiasm and assists in solving puzzles.

3 Wednesday
2nd ♏︎
Color: White

The Batu Caves in Malaysia hold splendid Hindu shrines.

4 Thursday
2nd ♏︎
☽ v/c 7:36 am
☽ enters ♐︎ 1:17 pm
Color: Purple

☺ Friday
2nd ♐︎
Full Moon 3:12 pm
Color: Rose

Strong Sun Moon
Lunar Eclipse 3:12 pm, 15° ♐︎ 34'

Set in Eastern Daylight Time (EDT)

Full Moon in Sagittarius

Sagittarius is the Visionary, the Truth Teller, the Seeker. This Full Moon underlines the archetypal Quest, and the first steps taken on the hero's journey. This Moon coincides with a lunar eclipse and is a good time to step out of our comfort zones and expand the boundaries of what is possible in our lives. It is a time to make a bid for freedom, to shake off the shackles of the expectations of others, and to envision a world of adventure, learning, and exploration. Clarify your goals and let the arrows of truth hit their mark. Sagittarius is connected to Artemis, goddess of the hunt and the Moon, protector of wild spaces and young girls. She values her freedom and independence, yet she is also aligned with a philosophical, mystical aspect. This is a good time to work magic for rejecting the confines of the patriarchy, to claim independence and the courage to live as we decree.

Artemis, teach me to rewild myself. To hone my vision and step into uncharted places with the fearless confidence of the Seeker and the heart of the Mystic.

Guiding Goddesses: Artemis, Diana, Flidais, Fatna

—Danielle Blackwood

6 Saturday

3rd ♐
☽ v/c 12:10 am
☽ enters ♑ 3:44 pm
Color: Gray

Gray is about neutrality and balance.
Wear it for buffering against extremes.

7 Sunday

3rd ♑
Color: Yellow

June

8 Monday

3rd ♑
☽ v/c 2:06 pm
☽ enters ♒ 8:54 pm
Color: White

9 Tuesday

3rd ♒
Color: Maroon

*If the candle won't light, it means a spell can't
help gain what you want; seek another path.*

10 Wednesday

3rd ♒
☽ v/c 10:35 am
Color: Brown

Celtic Tree Month of Oak begins

11 Thursday

3rd ♒
☽ enters ♓ 5:32 am
Color: Green

12 Friday

3rd ♓
Color: Coral

*The sweetness of honeysuckle incense
attracts friendship and admiration.*

◑ **Saturday**
3rd ♓
4th quarter 2:24 am
☽ v/c 8:45 am
☽ enters ♈ 5:03 pm
Color: Black

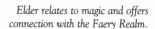

*Elder relates to magic and offers
connection with the Faery Realm.*

14 **Sunday**
4th ♈
Color: Gold

Flag Day

June

15 Monday

4th ♈
☽ v/c 8:49 pm
Color: Gray

Myrtle is a tree of love and peace.

16 Tuesday

4th ♈
☽ enters ♉ 5:35 am
Color: White

17 Wednesday

4th ♉
Color: Yellow

18 Thursday

4th ♉
☿ Rℛ 12:59 am
☽ v/c 8:02 am
☽ enters ♊ 5:00 pm
Color: Crimson

Mercury retrograde until July 12

19 Friday

4th ♊
Color: Pink

*Pink deals in subtlety and feelings. Use hot pink for mature
attraction or baby pink for innocence and friendship.*

Midsummer and the Sun

We celebrate the glory of the God at his peak strength and the pregnant Goddess's promise of abundance. Although the Goddess is, as always, important, this holiday focuses on the Sun and consequently on the God, so the connection to the Sun tarot card is obvious. The young child on a white horse symbolizes innocence, openness, and power. The red banner swirling from the sky to the earth reminds us that we are connected to the same vital life force that fuels all life, both physical and spiritual. Litha and the Sun card are both relatively simple, especially compared to the other holidays and their cards. The first fruits of summer are ripening. The atmosphere is languid but expectant. Meditate on the Sun to enhance enjoyment of the sweetness of nature, a foreshadowing of the rich abundance to come. Relish the beauty and delight all around. The Sun is warm, the fruit is sweet, and no one is in a rush. Everyday moments are dripping with pleasure. There is a feeling of success and accomplishment without stress or strife. Life is good simply because it is good.

—Barbara Moore

---

20 Saturday

4th ♊
☉ enters ♋ 5:44 pm
☽ v/c 5:48 pm
Color: Indigo

Midsummer/Litha/Summer Solstice
Sun enters Cancer

☽ Sunday

4th ♊
☽ enters ♋ 2:02 am
New Moon 2:41 am
Color: Orange

Father's Day
Solar Eclipse 2:41 am, 0° ♐ 21'

June

22 Monday
1st ♋
Color: Silver

23 Tuesday
1st ♋
Ψ Rx 12:31 am
☽ v/c 3:20 am
☽ enters ♌ 8:33 am
Color: Scarlet

24 Wednesday
1st ♌
☽ v/c 1:34 am
Color: Topaz

"The Universe is but one vast Symbol of God." —Thomas Carlyle

25 Thursday
1st ♌
♀ D 2:48 am
☽ enters ♍ 1:05 pm
Color: Turquoise

26 Friday
1st ♍
Color: White

Set in Eastern Daylight Time (EDT)

Iced Mint Tea

At Midsummer we reach the point of greatest light, when the power of the Sun imbues herbs with special magical and healing properties. For the Romans, mint was a symbol of hospitality, so why not share this reviving and stimulating drink with friends? It makes the perfect post-ritual brew.

2 bags black tea
3 sprigs mint
2 cups boiling water
Ice cubes
Sugar or honey to taste
Lemon slices
Additional mint sprigs to garnish

Put the 2 teabags and the 3 sprigs of mint into a teapot and pour on the boiling water. Infuse 3–4 minutes. Strain and cool. Pour into glasses with ice and sweeten to taste. Garnish with a slice of lemon and sprigs of mint.

—Anna Franklin

27 Saturday

1st ♍
☽ v/c 4:02 pm
☽ enters ♎ 4:16 pm
♂ enters ♈ 9:45 pm
Color: Blue

○ Sunday

1st ♎
2nd quarter 4:16 am
Color: Amber

Divination stones include jet, moonstone, and obsidian.

July 2020

S	M	T	W
			1
☺ *Blessing Moon* *Lunar Eclipse*	6	7	8
◖ *Mercury Direct*	13	14	15
19	☽	21	22 *Sun enters Leo*
26	●	28	29
2	3	4	5

T	F	S	Notes
2	3	4 Independence Day	
9	10	11	
16	17	18	
23	24	25	
30	31	1	
6	7	8	

June/July

29 Monday
2nd ♎
☽ v/c 9:02 am
☽ enters ♏ 6:48 pm
Color: Ivory

30 Tuesday
2nd ♏
Color: Gray

*Chew celery seed to boost
mental abilities and psychic powers.*

1 Wednesday
2nd ♏
♄ enters ♑ 7:37 pm
☽ v/c 9:20 pm
☽ enters ♐ 9:21 pm
Color: Brown

Canada Day

2 Thursday
2nd ♐
Color: Green

*A candle exploding, holder breaking, or other dramatic end means a
higher power has vetoed the spell; cleansing and meditation is advisable.*

3 Friday
2nd ♐
☽ v/c 9:06 am
Color: Purple

Set in Eastern Daylight Time (EDT)

Full Moon in Capricorn

The Full Moon in Capricorn delivers the second lunar eclipse in a row, and highlights themes of perseverance, accountability, and commitment. Capricorn is aligned with the archetype of the Elder and represents our psychic ancestral bones, as well as the stories and DNA that are passed down to us. It is a good time to work with ancestral magic and traditional folk magic. Capricorn is the Crone, the Wisewoman, the mentor. Capricorn medicine does not skip steps: it requires putting in the time and does not view shortcuts favorably. This Full Moon will show us in no uncertain terms where we have been coasting or living in denial. It will shine a light on where we need to step up to the plate and commit to the long view.

Hecate, Goddess of the Crossroads, lift your torch and light the path so that I may understand the patterns of the past in order to make the wisest choices for my next chapter.

Guiding Goddesses: Frau Holle, the Cailleach, Baba Yaga, Hecate

—Danielle Blackwood

---

4 Saturday

2nd ♐
☽ enters ♑ 12:48 am
Color: Blue

Independence Day

☻ Sunday

2nd ♑
Full Moon 12:44 am
Color: Gold

Blessing Moon
Lunar Eclipse, 12:44 am, 13° ♑ 38'

July

6 Monday
3rd ♑
☽ v/c 5:35 am
☽ enters ♒ 6:08 am
Color: Silver

*The otter brings joy and agility, a helpful guide
for water sports or people who need to cheer up.*

7 Tuesday
3rd ♒
☽ v/c 12:37 am
Color: Black

8 Wednesday
3rd ♒
☽ enters ♓ 2:13 pm
Color: Yellow

Celtic Tree Month of Holly begins

9 Thursday
3rd ♓
Color: Purple

Purple brings empowerment and wisdom. It is the color of elders.

10 Friday
3rd ♓
☽ v/c 11:49 pm
Color: Pink

Lemongrass Essential Oil

Lemongrass energizes the mind and brings positivity and brightness to the emotions. It helps us connect with our family, community, friends, and coworkers in the most nourishing and harmonious of ways. Inhale it before a party or gathering or anytime you'd like to honestly enjoy socializing and mingling with others. A popular ingredient in herbal insect repellents, lemongrass can be diffused or worn (in a carrier oil) to prevent bug bites. Similarly, it can facilitate a smoother flow through life by warding off minor irritations and hassles.

Additionally, lemongrass vibrates at the frequency of a healthy and balanced solar plexus chakra. It can help us reclaim and own our sense of personal power by reminding us of the many aspects of our lives over which we have control. This, in turn, can help alleviate both depression and anxiety and can reawaken us to our magical power. Lemongrass enhances claircognizance. If this is one of your natural intuitive gifts (or if you'd like it to be), inhale lemongrass before and during intuitive work.

—Tess Whitehurst

---

11 Saturday

3rd ♓
☽ enters ♈ 1:06 am
⚷ ℞ 5:09 pm
Color: Indigo

Indigo is the color of midnight and cosmic energy. Wear it for magical workings.

☽ Sunday

3rd ♈
☿ D 4:26 am
4th quarter 7:29 pm
Color: Yellow

July

13 Monday
4th ♈
☽ v/c 11:54 am
☽ enters ♉ 1:34 pm
Color: Lavender

*Angkor Wat in Cambodia is a vast
complex of temples in the jungle.*

14 Tuesday
4th ♉
Color: Scarlet

*Sherida is the Mesopotamian goddess of
dawn. She greets each day with a smile.*

15 Wednesday
4th ♉
☽ v/c 11:21 pm
Color: White

16 Thursday
4th ♉
☽ enters ♊ 1:19 am
Color: Crimson

*"This planet is our home. Our life and hers
are interdependent." —Doreen Valiente*

17 Friday
4th ♊
☽ v/c 5:14 pm
Color: Coral

18 Saturday

4th ♊

☽ enters ♋ 10:24 am

Color: Gray

19 Sunday

4th ♋

Color: Amber

*Redbud represents the divine feminine
with healing of shame and damaged land.*

July

☽ Monday
4th ♋
New Moon 1:33 pm
☽ v/c 1:55 pm
☽ enters ♌ 4:16 pm
Color: White

21 Tuesday
1st ♌
☽ v/c 8:27 pm
Color: Maroon

*Dill improves discernment, making it easier to
distinguish between magic and superstition.*

22 Wednesday
1st ♌
☉ enters ♌ 4:37 am
☽ enters ♍ 7:40 pm
Color: Yellow

Sun enters Leo

23 Thursday
1st ♍
Color: Turquoise

24 Friday
1st ♍
☽ v/c 7:08 pm
☽ enters ♎ 9:54 pm
Color: Rose

*When the flame forms a crater in the candle instead of burning all
the wax, it signifies a weak or blocked casting unlikely to succeed.*

Set in Eastern Daylight Time (EDT)

Sage Essential Oil

A botanical wise one, sage comforts, calms, and helps keep our auras healthy and clean. Simply wafting a bottle of essential oil of sage beneath your nose, or diffusing the scent, brings the mind and emotions into greater equilibrium. Inhaling the scent helps mitigate night sweats, premenstrual challenges, and digestive issues. It's a good idea to keep a bottle of essential oil of sage with you as spiritual first aid: inhale the scent before making decisions and to dissolve away anxiety, fear, anger, stuck or heavy energy, or any sort of emotional or energetic upset.

An excellent ally for meditation, essential oil of sage can also be employed to anoint charms created for cleansing, clarity, health, focus, protection, and wisdom. Add 10 to 20 drops to a mister of spring water to create a smudge spray that will cleanse away negativity from a person, object, or space. Lightly anointing your doors and windows with olive oil containing a few drops of essential oil of sage will help ensure that only positive people and energies enter your space.

—Tess Whitehurst

---

25 Saturday

1st ♎︎
Color: Brown

A garter is a symbol of high rank worn around the thigh;
the number of buckles indicates successful coven hivings.

---

26 Sunday

1st ♎︎
☽ v/c 9:09 pm
Color: Orange

July/August

◯ Monday
1st ♎
☽ enters ♏ 12:12 am
2nd quarter 8:33 am
Color: Ivory

*Palm represents the divine masculine and
qualities such as fertility and victory.*

28 Tuesday
2nd ♏
Color: Gray

29 Wednesday
2nd ♏
☽ v/c 12:01 am
☽ enters ♐ 3:25 am
Color: Topaz

*In Africa, Nyiko is a spider god and culture
hero. Call on him for aid in heroic endeavors.*

30 Thursday
2nd ♐
☽ v/c 8:08 pm
Color: White

31 Friday
2nd ♐
☽ enters ♑ 7:58 am
Color: Pink

Lammas and the Devil

The first of three harvest festivals, Lammas recognizes the sacrifice of the Oak King to feed the earth. While we are grateful for the harvest, we know that it comes with a price—the eventual death of the God and the coming of darkness. As the end of the growing season draws closer, there is an air of celebration and wild abandon, similar to some aspects of the Devil tarot card. This card represents enjoyment of the physical world, taking chances,

and sometimes taking risks that have a high cost. During Lammas, games are played, wagers made, and bread and beer enjoyed. The Devil card is often associated with the god Pan and hence is an appropriate match for this holiday, although the beverage of choice is more often made of grain than grapes. Lammas has an almost "eat, drink, and be merry, for tomorrow we die" sensibility. There is utter enjoyment without thinking about putting anything by for the future. There will be consequences, but in this moment, work with the Devil card to focus on celebrating the joys of the physical world. There will be time enough to think about the future.

—Barbara Moore

---

1 Saturday

2nd ♑
Color: Blue

Lammas/Lughnasadh

---

2 Sunday

2nd ♑
☽ v/c 9:59 am
☽ enters ♒ 2:11 pm
Color: Amber

A cape is a loose, open garment without a hood often used to indicate ritual role.

August 2020

S	M	T	W
2	😊	4	5
	Corn Moon		
9	10	◐	12
16	17	🌙	19
23	24	◐	26
30	31	1	2

T	F	S	Notes
		1 Lammas	
6	7	8	
13	14	15	
20	21	22 Sun enters Virgo	
27	28	29	
3	4	5	

August

☺ **Monday**
2nd ≈
Full Moon 11:59 am
Color: Gray

Corn Moon

4 Tuesday
3rd ≈
☽ v/c 5:45 pm
☽ enters ♓ 10:28 pm
☿ enters ♌ 11:32 pm
Color: White

5 Wednesday
3rd ♓
Color: Yellow

Celtic Tree Month of Hazel begins

6 Thursday
3rd ♓
Color: Turquoise

Lammas crossquarter day (Sun reaches 15° Leo)

7 Friday
3rd ♓
☽ v/c 8:53 am
☽ enters ♈ 9:05 am
♀ enters ♋ 11:21 am
Color: Purple

Set in Eastern Daylight Time (EDT)

Full Moon in Aquarius

The Full Moon in Aquarius awakens us personally and collectively to the need for social change. Aquarius resonates with the archetypes of the Rebel, the Revolutionary, and the Wild Card. Aquarius is a nonconformist breaker of rules and creator of new paradigms. This Full Moon calls us to authenticity, to being true to ourselves and to our visions for social justice. We gather to create change, make our voices heard, and champion those causes that speak to our highest ideals. This is a good time for working magic for social change, activism, and overcoming systemic oppression. This Full Moon is also a time to open the gateway to fresh creative vision. The Irish goddess Brigit is connected to Aquarius, and poets, storytellers, musicians, and artists would appeal to her for the divine spark of inspiration.

Brigit, Bright One, ignite my creative fire and enchant my work with your vision. Help me refill my well and be open to divine inspiration.

Guiding Goddesses: Brigit, Lilith, Nut, Tien-Mu

—Danielle Blackwood

---

8 Saturday

3rd ♈
Color: Black

---

9 Sunday

3rd ♈
☽ v/c 3:50 pm
☽ enters ♉ 9:28 pm
Color: Orange

White smoke from an extinguished candle indicates positive energy, and you'll probably get what you asked for.

August

10 Monday
3rd ♉
Color: Silver

"Ask stones and plants to reveal their powers—and listen." —Scott Cunningham

○ Tuesday
3rd ♉
4th quarter 12:45 pm
Color: Red

Laufakanaa is a Tongan god of bananas. Ask his aid in protecting or procuring them.

12 Wednesday
4th ♉
☽ v/c 3:55 am
☽ enters ♊ 9:46 am
Color: Brown

13 Thursday
4th ♊
Color: Green

14 Friday
4th ♊
☽ v/c 7:19 am
☽ enters ♋ 7:35 pm
Color: Coral

For beauty, wear amber or cat's eye.

Ratatouille (Vegan)

1 large eggplant
1 large onion
2 large bell peppers
3 zucchini
6 medium-size fresh tomatoes
⅔ cup olive oil
3 cloves garlic, crushed
1 tsp. fresh thyme leaves
1 can plum tomatoes
Salt and pepper
1 T. fresh basil leaves, shredded
Zest of ½ lemon

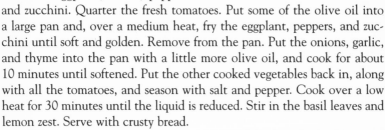

Slice the eggplant, onion, peppers and zucchini. Quarter the fresh tomatoes. Put some of the olive oil into a large pan and, over a medium heat, fry the eggplant, peppers, and zucchini until soft and golden. Remove from the pan. Put the onions, garlic, and thyme into the pan with a little more olive oil, and cook for about 10 minutes until softened. Put the other cooked vegetables back in, along with all the tomatoes, and season with salt and pepper. Cook over a low heat for 30 minutes until the liquid is reduced. Stir in the basil leaves and lemon zest. Serve with crusty bread.

What better way to use fresh seasonal vegetables than this healthy stew?

—Anna Franklin

---

15 Saturday

4th ♋
♅ Rx 10:25 am
Color: Indigo

---

16 Sunday

4th ♋
☽ v/c 7:59 pm
Color: Amber

August

17 Monday
4th ♋
☽ enters ♌ 1:38 am
Color: Lavender

☽ Tuesday
4th ♌
New Moon 10:42 pm
Color: Gray

Acacia grants protection and teaches symbiosis.

19 Wednesday
1st ♌
☽ v/c 1:38 am
☽ enters ♍ 4:20 am
☿ enters ♍ 9:30 pm
Color: White

20 Thursday
1st ♍
☽ v/c 11:37 pm
Color: Crimson

Islamic New Year (begins at sundown on August 19)

21 Friday
1st ♍
☽ enters ♎ 5:16 am
Color: Pink

Priests often wear a necklace of antler and wood.

Set in Eastern Daylight Time (EDT)

Vetiver Essential Oil

Vetiver is a deeply grounding and centering oil. Magical and spiritual practitioners who can't stand patchouli often find it a worthy substitute, though it's a unique and powerful oil in its own right. It has a singular ability to disperse blocks to financial abundance. Try anointing your wallet with vetiver regularly to open up to a generous financial flow.

When the body needs nourishment—after illness or any sort of health challenge—vetiver is an excellent ally, promoting hunger and the desire for healthy foods and activities. It supports the balance and strengthening of the skin, bones, and internal organs, and bolsters hormone and glandular wellness. For a health charm, tie an acorn in a scrap of green cotton fabric and anoint it with vetiver oil.

It's a good idea to diffuse vetiver to combat burnout and help you regain your natural energy and enthusiasm. Those healing from addiction can also benefit from vetiver's ability to realign the body, mind, and spirit with their natural state of balance and well-being.

—Tess Whitehurst

22 Saturday

1st ♎
☉ enters ♍ 11:45 am
Color: Brown

Sun enters Virgo

23 Sunday

1st ♎
☽ v/c 12:20 am
☽ enters ♏ 6:16 am
Color: Yellow

August

24 Monday
1st ♏
Color: Ivory

Black smoke from an extinguished candle indicates negative energy, and cleansing is advisable.

○ Tuesday
1st ♏
☽ v/c 2:27 am
☽ enters ♐ 8:49 am
2nd quarter 1:58 pm
Color: Scarlet

Lunar jasmine has a potent floral fragrance with watery notes, ideal for meditation and water magic.

26 Wednesday
2nd ♐
Color: Topaz

27 Thursday
2nd ♐
☽ v/c 8:00 am
☽ enters ♑ 1:37 pm
Color: Turquoise

28 Friday
2nd ♑
Color: Rose

Cenote Sagrado in Mexico is a natural sinkhole filled with water, a site of rituals and offerings where jewelry, pottery, and other artifacts are found.

29 Saturday

2nd ♑
☽ v/c 3:31 pm
☽ enters ♒ 8:37 pm
Color: Black

The baobab is a world tree that
connects the material and spiritual realms.

30 Sunday

2nd ♒
Color: Gold

September 2020

S	M	T	W
		1	☻ Harvest Moon
6	7 Labor Day	8	9
13	14	15	16
20	21	22 Mabon / Fall Equinox Sun enters Libra	☾
27	28	29	30
4	5	6	7

T	F	S	
3	4	5	**Notes**
○	11	12	
☽	18	19	
24	25	26	
1	2	3	
8	9	10	

31 Monday
2nd ≈
Color: Silver

*"A room without books is as a body
without a soul." —Sir John Lubbock*

1 Tuesday
2nd ≈
☽ v/c 12:56 am
☽ enters ♓ 5:34 am
Color: Black

☺ Wednesday
2nd ♓
Full Moon 1:22 am
Color: Yellow

Celtic Tree Month of Vine begins
Harvest Moon

3 Thursday
3rd ♓
☽ v/c 10:34 am
☽ enters ♈ 4:22 pm
Color: Purple

*Eingana is the dreamtime snake goddess of Australia,
who gave birth to humans and water creatures.*

4 Friday
3rd ♈
Color: White

Full Moon in Pisces

The Full Moon in Pisces illuminates the mystery behind the veil of the High Priestess. Pisces is connected to the archetypes of the Mystic, the Dreamer, the Poet, and the Witch. This Full Moon is a threshold to the Otherworld, and a good time for divination, mediumship, and working with spirits. It is also a powerful time for magical workings that include trancework, dreamwork, and connecting with the water element. Creative inspiration and intuitive knowing are enhanced by the light of this Moon, but we can just as easily feel overwhelmed and wish to pull the covers over our heads and escape. Kwan Yin, the Buddhist goddess of compassion, is one deity that embodies the Pisces archetype. It is said that just calling or chanting her name will protect one from harm. One word of advice with this lunation: keep your feet and maintain healthy boundaries so you don't get swept away by the currents.

Kwan Yin, I call on you to remind me to have compassion not only for others but for myself.

Guiding Goddesses: Kwan Yin, Yemaya, Sedna, Oshun

—Danielle Blackwood

---

5 Saturday

3rd ♈
☿ enters ♎ 3:46 pm
Color: Brown

Brown is the color of earth and animal magic. It appears in fur, leather, wood, and stone—all good for natural spells.

---

6 Sunday

3rd ♈
☽ v/c 12:45 am
♀ enters ♌ 3:22 am
☽ enters ♉ 4:43 am
Color: Amber

September

7 Monday
3rd ♉
Color: White

Labor Day
Labour Day (Canada)

8 Tuesday
3rd ♉
☽ v/c 8:47 am
☽ enters ♊ 5:28 pm
Color: Scarlet

*Amber incense has a musky floral scent that
works well for love spells and temple incense.*

9 Wednesday
3rd ♊
♂ ℞ 6:22 pm
Color: Topaz

Mars retrograde until November 13

☽ Thursday
3rd ♊
4th quarter 5:26 am
Color: Green

11 Friday
4th ♊
☽ v/c 12:48 am
☽ enters ♋ 4:23 am
Color: Purple

Set in Eastern Daylight Time (EDT)

12 Saturday

4th ♋
♃ D 8:41 pm
Color: Gray

If the candle flame blazes and dances,
the spell energy is strong but chaotic.

13 Sunday

4th ♋
☽ v/c 8:05 am
☽ enters ♌ 11:32 am
Color: Yellow

September

14 Monday
4th ♌
Color: Ivory

*You can ground energy with hematite,
moonstone, or black tourmaline.*

15 Tuesday
4th ♌
☽ v/c 11:09 am
☽ enters ♍ 2:37 pm
Color: Red

16 Wednesday
4th ♍
Color: White

☽ Thursday
4th ♍
New Moon 7:00 am
☽ v/c 7:42 am
☽ enters ♎ 2:56 pm
Color: Turquoise

*Sweet and fruity, strawberry incense
encourages generosity and affection.*

18 Friday
1st ♎
Color: Rose

Apple Amber

Pack of frozen shortcrust pastry,
   defrosted
1½ cups cooking apples
¾ cup moist brown sugar
½ cup butter
2 eggs, separated
Grated zest and juice of ½ lemon
Pinch of cinnamon
Pinch of ground cloves
½ cup superfine (caster) sugar

Line a pie dish with the pastry. Peel
and chop the apples and cook them
in a pan with the brown sugar and
1 tablespoon water until tender. Then push the mixture through a sieve.
Return the pulp to the pan and add the lemon juice and zest, along with
the spices. Warm through, adding the butter and egg yolks, and cook gen-
tly until it begins to thicken. Pour into your pastry crust. Bake at 350°F
until set, about 20 minutes. Meanwhile, whisk the egg whites with the
superfine sugar until the mixture forms stiff peaks. Spoon onto the pie,
sealing it to the edges of the pie crust, and return the pie to the oven for
10 minutes.

—Anna Franklin

---

19 Saturday

1st ♎
☽ v/c 10:29 am
☽ enters ♏ 2:33 pm
Color: Blue

Rosh Hashanah (begins at sundown on September 18)

---

20 Sunday

1st ♏
Color: Orange

*The pelican is opportunistic and gregarious,
a great spirit animal for entrepreneurs.*

September

21 Monday
1st ♏
☽ v/c 2:13 pm
☽ enters ♐ 3:32 pm
Color: Silver

UN International Day of Peace

22 Tuesday
1st ♐
☉ enters ♎ 9:31 am
Color: Maroon

Mabon/Fall Equinox
Sun enters Libra

◑ Wednesday
1st ♐
☽ v/c 1:31 pm
☽ enters ♑ 7:16 pm
2nd quarter 9:55 pm
Color: Yellow

24 Thursday
2nd ♑
Color: Crimson

For money spells, choose from
aventurine, emerald, pearl, ruby, or topaz.

25 Friday
2nd ♑
☽ v/c 11:36 pm
Color: Pink

Set in Eastern Daylight Time (EDT)

Mabon and Justice

The God and the Goddess return to the underworld as we celebrate the second harvest and main bounty of the year. Our minds turn to preparing for winter. Without modern food preservation techniques, storing food for winter had a different urgency, one that we probably cannot imagine but still serves as a metaphor. As in the Justice tarot card, the consequences of our actions and their effects on the future are paramount in our minds. Will what we have done be enough to sustain us through the season of darkness? At Mabon, we also focus on forgiveness, a kind of divine justice that goes beyond human justice, one threaded through with mercy. Accept the Justice card's invitation to consider the long-term effects of your thoughts, feelings, and actions. You are, after all, beginning to reap what you have sown. In the midst of expressions of gratitude for the abundance of the world, think about molding the future. We have some time left to honor our responsibility to the cycle of life and to prepare our lives, both mundane and spiritual, for the cold, dark days to come.

—Barbara Moore

26 Saturday
2nd ♑
☽ enters ♒ 2:08 am
Color: Indigo

27 Sunday
2nd ♒
☿ enters ♏ 3:41 am
Color: Gold

The Dampier Rock Art precinct in Australia covers many square miles with over a million petroglyphs and stone arrangements.

October 2020

S	M	T	W
4	5	6	7
11	12	13 Mercury Retrograde	14
18	19	20	21
25	26	27	28
1	2	3	4

T	F	S	Notes
☺	2	3	
Blood Moon			
8	◑	10	
15	☽	17	
22	◐	24	
Sun enters Scorpio			
29	30	☺	
		Samhain Halloween Blue Moon	
5	6	7	

September/October

28 Monday

2nd ♒
☽ v/c 3:18 am
☽ enters ♓ 11:34 am
Color: Gray

Yom Kippur (begins at sundown on September 27)

29 Tuesday

2nd ♓
♄ D 1:11 am
Color: Scarlet

30 Wednesday

2nd ♓
☽ v/c 1:30 pm
☽ enters ♈ 10:47 pm
Color: Brown

Celtic Tree Month of Ivy begins

☺ Thursday

2nd ♈
Full Moon 5:05 pm
Color: Green

Blood Moon

2 Friday

3rd ♈
♀ enters ♍ 4:48 pm
Color: Coral

For wealth, anoint a buckeye with money oil,
wrap it in a dollar bill, and carry it in your pocket.

Set in Eastern Daylight Time (EDT)

Full Moon in Aries

The Aries Full Moon lights up the night sky, underlining themes of passion and courage. Aries is the archetype of the Warrior and helps us stand our ground and assert ourselves. This is a good time for magical work for protection, defining boundaries, and channeling righteous anger toward needed change. Aries magic is potent when we need to take a stance. Tapping into Aries energy rekindles our spark and gives us the motivation to make something happen, and this Full Moon can inspire us with the courage to begin again. The Aries Full Moon is a catalyst that encourages us go after what is important to us and can help restore our vitality. The Irish goddess Macha is a deity who exemplifies Aries. As such, she relates to protection, setting boundaries, sovereignty, and honor.

Macha, help me embrace my inner Warrior, so I may know when it is time to be fierce and to stand up for what I know is right.

Guiding Goddesses: Macha, Freya, the Morrigan, Pele

—Danielle Blackwood

---

3 Saturday

3rd ♈
☽ v/c 1:47 am
☽ enters ♉ 11:12 am
Color: Blue

Sukkot begins (at sundown on October 2)

---

4 Sunday

3rd ♉
♀ D 9:32 am
Color: Yellow

---

5 Monday

3rd ♉
☽ v/c 2:41 pm
Color: Ivory

6 Tuesday

3rd ♉
☽ enters ♊ 12:03 am
Color: Gray

*Woodsy and spicy, sandalwood
incense consecrates and heals.*

7 Wednesday

3rd ♊
☽ v/c 9:57 pm
Color: Yellow

Priestesses often wear a necklace of amber and jet.

8 Thursday

3rd ♊
☽ enters ♋ 11:45 am
Color: Purple

◑ Friday

3rd ♋
4th quarter 8:40 pm
Color: Rose

Sukkot ends

Clove Essential Oil

Inhaling the scent of clove essential oil fills us with confidence and well-being. It grounds us solidly in the earthly realm while rousing our creativity and joy. Naturally, these qualities lend themselves the magical intentions of courage, abundance, strength, health, happiness, personal power, and success. Diffuse the essential oil while recuperating from stress, exhaustion, or fatigue to help recharge and recalibrate your energy.

By bolstering the heart and fortifying the will, clove makes for a valuable ally during major life changes, such as moving to a new city, starting a new job or business, or rediscovering yourself after a breakup. For this purpose, diffuse the essential oil in your space or create a heart-bolstering charm by nestling a bloodstone heart in a small dish of whole cloves and dropping a few drops of clove essential oil onto the cloves regularly to keep the scent and magic strong. This scent also awakens and focuses the mind. Inhale it before taking a test, while studying, or to stimulate creative thought.

—Tess Whitehurst

---

10 Saturday

4th ♋
☽ v/c 12:04 pm
☽ enters ♌ 8:24 pm
Color: Indigo

*The armadillo grants protection
and supports nonattachment.*

---

11 Sunday

4th ♌
Color: Orange

October

12 Monday
4th ♌
☽ v/c 10:29 am
Color: Lavender

Columbus Day
Indigenous Peoples' Day
Thanksgiving Day (Canada)

13 Tuesday
4th ♌
☽ enters ♍ 12:56 am
☿ Rℵ 9:05 pm
Color: Red

Mercury retrograde until November 3

14 Wednesday
4th ♍
☽ v/c 6:47 pm
Color: White

15 Thursday
4th ♍
☽ enters ♎ 1:54 am
Color: Turquoise

*"At heart we are all powerful, beautiful, and capable of
changing the world with our bare hands." —Dianne Sylvan*

☽ Friday
4th ♎
New Moon 3:31 pm
☽ v/c 6:11 pm
Color: Pink

Set in Eastern Daylight Time (EDT)

17 Saturday

1st ♎
☽ enters ♏ 1:05 am
Color: Black

Fufluns is the Etruscan god of feasts and festivals. Ask his blessing for a successful potluck.

18 Sunday

1st ♏
☽ v/c 5:43 pm
Color: Yellow

October

19 Monday
1st ♏
☽ enters ♐ 12:43 am
Color: White

*Bear Lodge, or Devils Tower, in the United States is a place
where the Crow people hold ceremonies, including the Sun Dance.*

20 Tuesday
1st ♐
☽ v/c 11:38 pm
Color: Black

21 Wednesday
1st ♐
☽ enters ♑ 2:44 am
Color: Topaz

22 Thursday
1st ♑
☉ enters ♏ 7:00 pm
☽ v/c 9:35 pm
Color: Purple

Sun enters Scorpio

○ Friday
1st ♑
☽ v/c 12:35 am
☽ enters ♒ 8:17 am
2nd quarter 9:23 am
Color: White

Samhain and the Moon

At Samhain, the Great Goddess reigns in the form of the Crone and the Great God in the form of the Horned God or the Lord of Death. We honor ancestors and prepare for a time of reflection. The Moon tarot card also suggests a time of reflection, as the Moon reflects the light of the Sun. Part of the spiritual work of the dark time of the year is clearing out that which no longer serves, which usually includes facing fears and difficult truths, our inner  dragons. The crayfish in the Moon card represents these fears rising up in the unconscious. The Moon card is also associated with divination, strong spiritual connections, and communication between realms. Samhain, a time when the veil between worlds is thin, is also a time for divinatory activities and ancestor work. The card features a lot of water, representing the deep and sometimes turbulent waters of the soul. Dive deeply and submerge yourself in the Moon. Find your way through these deeps and discover the gifts that will shape you as you continue your journey.

—Barbara Moore

---

24 Saturday

2nd ♒
☽ v/c 5:54 pm
Color: Gray

---

25 Sunday

2nd ♒
☽ enters ♓ 5:18 pm
Color: Gold

October/November

26 Monday
2nd ♓
Color: Silver

*Healing poppets, pillows, or sachets may be
stuffed with eucalyptus for a swift recovery.*

27 Tuesday
2nd ♓
☽ v/c 8:46 pm
☿ enters ♎ 9:33 pm
♀ enters ♎ 9:41 pm
Color: Scarlet

28 Wednesday
2nd ♓
☽ enters ♈ 4:45 am
Color: White

Celtic Tree Month of Reed begins

29 Thursday
2nd ♈
Color: Crimson

30 Friday
2nd ♈
☽ v/c 12:12 pm
☽ enters ♉ 5:19 pm
Color: Purple

*If the candle flame is weak and sputtery,
the spell energy is feeble and erratic.*

Set in Eastern Daylight Time (EDT)

Full Moon in Taurus

This is the Full Moon magical folk have been awaiting since 2001! The Taurus Full Moon occurs on Samhain this year! Taurus resonates with the themes of resources, pleasure, beauty, earthly delights, hedonism, and the sensual aspect of sex. Taurus is connected to the experience of being embodied. Sex magic is a powerful way to channel both the Full Moon in Taurus and the Sun in Scorpio. Taurus is aligned with Aphrodite Pandemos, the sensual, earthy fertility goddess associated with the pleasure of physical love, as well as the goddess of courtesans and hetaerae. In addition to Samhain-centered magic, this is also a good time for magical work that centers around cultivating right livelihood, manifestation, and financial security. Working with the earth element, herbs, dance, and drumming makes our magic extra potent now.

Aphrodite Pandemos, help me experience wild joy in my body and accept pleasure, enjoyment, and abundance as my birthright.

Guiding Goddesses: Aphrodite Pandemos, Gaia, Annapurna, Ixcacao
—Danielle Blackwood

☺ Saturday

2nd ♉
Full Moon 10:49 am
Color: Brown

Samhain/Halloween
Blue Moon

---

1 Sunday

3rd ♉
☽ v/c 9:29 pm
Color: Orange

All Saints' Day
Daylight Saving Time ends at 2 am

November 2020

S	M	T	W
1 Daylight Saving Time ends at 2 am	2	3 Election Day (general) Mercury Direct	4
◖	9	10	11
☽	16	17	18
22	23	24	25
29	☺ Mourning Moon Lunar Eclipse	1	2
6	7	8	9

T	F	S	Notes
5	6	7	
12	13	14	
19	20	☾ Sun enters Sagittarius	
26 Thanksgiving Day	27	28	
3	4	5	
10	11	12	

November

2 Monday

3rd ♉
☽ enters ♊ 5:00 am
Color: White

3 Tuesday

3rd ♊
☿ D 12:50 pm
Color: Black

Election Day (general)

4 Wednesday

3rd ♊
☽ v/c 8:49 am
☽ enters ♋ 4:45 pm
Color: Yellow

To gain courage, carry amethyst, bloodstone, or tiger's eye.

5 Thursday

3rd ♋
Color: Turquoise

6 Friday

3rd ♋
☽ v/c 8:27 pm
Color: Pink

Set in Eastern Standard Time (EST)

Soul Cakes

3½ cups all-purpose flour
1 tsp. pumpkin spice (mixed spice)
¾ cup butter
¾ cup superfine (caster) sugar
3 egg yolks
½ cup currants or raisins
Milk

Sift the flour and spice. Cream the butter and sugar in a bowl, then beat in the egg yolks. Add the flour and spice mixture and the raisins. Add enough milk to form a soft dough.

Flatten, cut into small cakes, and mark with a cross. Place on a greased baking tray and bake at 350°F degrees until golden brown, about 10 to 15 minutes.

From the Middle Ages until the 1930s, when the practice gradually died out, soul cakes were traditionally made for All Hallow's Eve in England and given out to children and beggars who came to the door, singing and pleading for treats:

A soul! a soul! a soul cake! Please, good missus, a soul cake!

We use soul cakes in our Samhain ritual, putting them out as offerings for the ancestors.

—Anna Franklin

---

7 Saturday

3rd ♋
☽ enters ♌ 2:18 am
Color: Blue

Samhain crossquarter day (Sun reaches 15° Scorpio)

◯ Sunday

3rd ♌
4th quarter 8:46 am
Color: Amber

*Cinnamon is a fiery, masculine incense
with the ability to raise or quell desire.*

November

9 Monday
4th ♌
☽ v/c 6:05 am
☽ enters ♍ 8:30 am
Color: Silver

*The creator god Barong comes from
Southeast Asia. He appears as a lion.*

10 Tuesday
4th ♍
☿ enters ♏ 4:55 pm
Color: Maroon

11 Wednesday
4th ♍
☽ v/c 5:58 am
☽ enters ♎ 11:09 am
Color: Brown

Veterans Day
Remembrance Day (Canada)

12 Thursday
4th ♎
Color: Crimson

*A cloak is a loose, open garment with a hood
useful for concealment and dramatic appearance.*

13 Friday
4th ♎
☽ v/c 6:32 am
☽ enters ♏ 11:19 am
♂ D 7:36 pm
Color: White

Douglas Fir Essential Oil

As if smelling just like a Yule tree weren't enough, Douglas fir essential oil attracts health, wealth, happiness, and luck. Its sweet freshness reminds us that we are divine, lovable, and worthy of every wonderful thing. Diffuse the scent while cleaning to invite blessings of prosperity and harmony into the home. Turn around a challenging string of luck by anointing a white candle with sunflower oil containing a few drops of Douglas fir and a few drops of peppermint. Set the intention to draw good luck, then light.

An excellent ally for the winter months, Douglas fir helps clear airways and bolster energy levels. Try diffusing it with eucalyptus and rosemary to receive these benefits. (This blend has the added benefit of bringing focus and clarity to the mind.) Help alleviate seasonal affective disorder, depression, or fatigue by keeping a bottle close and inhaling the scent as needed to boost your energy and harmonize your mood. You can also anoint a dollar bill with Douglas fir oil and place it in your wallet or purse to attract windfalls and help ensure that you will always have plenty to spare and share.

—Tess Whitehurst

14 Saturday
4th ♏
Color: Black

☽ Sunday
4th ♏
New Moon 12:07 am
☽ v/c 6:13 am
☽ enters ♐ 10:47 am
Color: Gold

Fir promotes abundance and aids shadow work.

November

16 Monday
1st ♐
Color: Gray

17 Tuesday
1st ♐
☽ v/c 2:55 am
☽ enters ♑ 11:35 am
Color: Red

*"The death of fear is in doing what you
fear to do." —Sequichie Comingdeer*

18 Wednesday
1st ♑
Color: Topaz

19 Thursday
1st ♑
☽ v/c 11:30 am
☽ enters ♒ 3:25 pm
Color: Purple

*The zebra is wild and free, yet interdependent within its
own herd, useful qualities to gain from a spirit animal.*

20 Friday
1st ♒
☽ v/c 7:49 pm
Color: Rose

☽ Saturday

1st ≈
♀ enters ♏ 8:22 am
☉ enters ♐ 3:40 pm
☽ enters ♓ 11:06 pm
2nd quarter 11:45 pm
Color: Brown

Sun enters Sagittarius

22 Sunday

2nd ♓
Color: Orange

Orange invites acceptance and
warmth. Use it for motivation.

November

23 Monday

2nd ♓
Color: Lavender

Wisteria overcomes obstacles and opens psychic abilities.

24 Tuesday

2nd ♓
☽ v/c 5:44 am
☽ enters ♈ 10:05 am
Color: Scarlet

25 Wednesday

2nd ♈
Color: White

Celtic Tree Month of Elder begins

26 Thursday

2nd ♈
☽ v/c 6:46 pm
☽ enters ♉ 10:43 pm
Color: Green

Thanksgiving Day (US)

27 Friday

2nd ♉
Color: Coral

Set in Eastern Standard Time (EST)

Patchouli Essential Oil

No essential oil grounds us in the physical realm and brings us into our senses quite like patchouli. When you feel anxious or ungrounded (i.e., like your energy is whipping around your head and shoulders while completely depriving your heart, belly, and feet of the feeling of being connected to the earth), inhale patchouli for an instant, potent, and reliable anchor.

This uncommon power of patchouli lends itself to the additional benefits of enhancing intimacy and attuning us to the frequency of abundant wealth. For either magical aim, wear patchouli and diffuse it regularly in your space.

While the earthly realm is often equated with the mundane, patchouli does not make this association. In fact, patchouli can help open you up to magical earth beings such as fairies, tree spirits, and spirit animals. Create a charm to do just that by tying a bloodstone into green or brown cotton fabric with hemp twine. Anoint it with patchouli and keep it with you during a meditative nature walk or inner shamanic journey.

—Tess Whitehurst

---

28 Saturday

2nd ♉
♆ D 7:36 pm
Color: Blue

> *"If you have time to breathe you have time to meditate."* —Buddhist monk Ajahn Amaro

---

29 Sunday

2nd ♉
☽ v/c 7:48 am
☽ enters ♊ 11:16 am
Color: Yellow

December 2020

S	M	T	W
		1	2
6	◑	8	9
13	☾ Solar Eclipse	15	16
20	◐ Yule / Winter Solstice Sun enters Capricorn	22	23
27	28	☺ Long Nights Moon	30
3	4	5	6

T	F	S	Notes
3	4	5	
10	11	12	
17	18	19	
24 Christmas Eve	25 Christmas Day	26	
31 New Year's Eve	1	2	
7	8	9	

☉ Monday
2nd ♊
Full Moon 4:30 am
☽ v/c 11:22 pm
Color: Ivory

Mourning Moon
Lunar Eclipse, 4:30 am, 8° ♊ 38'

1 Tuesday
3rd ♊
☿ enters ♐ 2:51 pm
☽ enters ♋ 10:33 pm
Color: Black

*The underworld goddess Setesuyara comes from
Southeast Asia. She is the consort of Batara-Kala.*

2 Wednesday
3rd ♋
Color: Yellow

3 Thursday
3rd ♋
Color: White

Erlik is the Finnish creator god. He enjoys mud and slime.

4 Friday
3rd ♋
☽ v/c 5:29 am
☽ enters ♌ 7:53 am
Color: Purple

Full Moon in Gemini

Coinciding with the last lunar eclipse of the year, the Full Moon in Gemini brings us to a new threshold of becoming. Gemini is connected to the archetypes of the Shape-shifter, the Storyteller, and the Walker between the Worlds. Gemini is associated with the magic of words, so it is a good time for magic workings that include spoken incantations, written spells, affirmations, or chanting. Gemini wisdom teaches us to see all sides of a given situation, and its association with Mercury, the psychopomp or divine messenger, facilitates travel between the worlds of the subconscious or spirit world to bring messages to the topside world. Butterfly Maiden, or Pahlik Mana, from the indigenous Hopi tribe is a goddess who resonates with the archetype of Gemini and represents the fluidity of transformation and renewal.

Butterfly Maiden, show me the wisdom in trusting the cycles of change and how to dance in the spaces between.

Guiding Goddesses: Butterfly Maiden, Sarasvati, Blodeuwedd, Psyche

—Danielle Blackwood

---

5 Saturday

3rd ♌
☽ v/c 5:28 pm
Color: Gray

Nan Madol in Micronesia is a basalt monument where Pohnpeian islanders worship the honored spirit of the land.

6 Sunday

3rd ♌
☽ enters ♍ 2:46 pm
Color: Orange

December

◯ Monday
3rd ♍
4th quarter 7:37 pm
Color: Silver

8 Tuesday
4th ♍
☽ v/c 5:35 pm
☽ enters ♎ 7:01 pm
Color: Scarlet

In South America, Guinechin is the god of stability.
He maintains equilibrium in the face of evil and chaos.

9 Wednesday
4th ♎
Color: White

10 Thursday

4th ♎
☽ v/c 7:56 pm
☽ enters ♏ 8:59 pm
Color: Crimson

Lavender incense is cleansing and
refreshing, good for air magic.

11 Friday

4th ♏
Color: Coral

Hanukkah begins (at sundown on December 10)

Set in Eastern Standard Time (EST)

Mincemeat Jam

5½ cups cooking apples
Juice and zest of 1 lemon
3 cups sultanas
¼ tsp. grated nutmeg
1 tsp. ground ginger
2 cups cold water
3½ cups sugar

Peel and chop the apples. Put in a heavy pan with the lemon juice and zest, sultanas, spices, and cold water. Bring to a simmering point and cook until the fruit is tender. Add the sugar, stirring well until dissolved. Bring to a fast boil for 20 minutes, stirring occasionally. Test for setting point by putting a little on a saucer, refrigerating for a couple of minutes, and pushing with your fingertip. When it wrinkles, the jam is ready.

In Britain, no Yuletide is complete without mince pies, individual little pastry pies filled with "mincemeat." There was a superstition that you should eat a mince pie every day of the Twelve Days of Christmas for twelve months of good health in the coming year. There is no actual meat involved, despite the name, though traditional mincemeat involves the use of suet or vegetarian suet. This jam is an easier option.

—Anna Franklin

12 Saturday

4th ♏
☽ v/c 8:58 pm
☽ enters ♐ 9:39 pm
Color: Indigo

Stones of wisdom include jade, sodalite, and sugilite.

13 Sunday

4th ♐
Color: Gold

December

☽ Monday
4th ♐
☽ v/c 11:17 am
New Moon 11:17 am
☽ enters ♑ 10:35 pm
Color: White

Solar Eclipse, 11:17 am, 23° ♐ 08'

15 Tuesday
1st ♑
♀ enters ♐ 11:21 am
☿ D 5:17 pm
Color: Maroon

As part of a sachet, xanthan gum banishes fear,
wards off negative influences, and promotes courage.

16 Wednesday
1st ♑
Color: Brown

17 Thursday
1st ♑
♄ enters ♒ 12:04 am
☽ v/c 12:34 am
☽ enters ♒ 1:27 am
Color: Turquoise

Vanilla incense is sweet and mellow.
Burn it to relax and release stress.

18 Friday
1st ♒
Color: Rose

Hanukkah ends

Set in Eastern Standard Time (EST)

19 Saturday

1st ≈
☽ v/c 3:45 am
☽ enters ♓ 7:39 am
♃ enters ≈ 8:07 am
Color: Black

A strong candle flame means
high, focused energy in a spell.

20 Sunday

1st ♓
☿ enters ♑ 6:07 pm
Color: Yellow

December

○ Monday

1st ♓
☉ enters ♑ 5:02 am
☽ v/c 5:25 am
☽ enters ♈ 5:32 pm
2nd quarter 6:41 pm
Color: Gray

Yule/Winter Solstice
Sun enters Capricorn

22 Tuesday

2nd ♈
Color: Red

23 Wednesday

2nd ♈
☽ v/c 5:51 pm
Color: Topaz

Between (Celtic Tree Month)

24 Thursday

2nd ♈
☽ enters ♉ 5:55 am
Color: Purple

Christmas Eve
Celtic Tree Month of Birch begins

25 Friday

2nd ♉
Color: Pink

Christmas Day

Set in Eastern Standard Time (EST)

Yule and Death

On the longest night of the year, the Great Mother gives birth to the Sun God. While it may seem odd to associate this celebration of the promise of new life with the Death card, doing so helps us think more broadly about Yule. Just as Yule is the longest period of darkness, Death represents the darkness before the dawn. One of Death's themes is endings, such as the end of the year or the releasing of things that no longer support the greatest good. Death can represent a crisis of faith while Yule is festival of faith. The Sun has not begun its return and in fact seems farther away than ever, but we believe the light will return. Meditate on this card as you assess your life. Focus on winnowing out that which no longer serves you. Allow the debris to break down, becoming fertile soil for future seeds to take root and find nourishment. Sometimes facing our darkest parts requires courage and a firm belief that we will not only survive but also make way for new life to grow.

—Barbara Moore

26 Saturday

2nd ☉
☽ v/c 6:32 am
☽ enters ♊ 6:33 pm
Color: Blue

Kwanzaa begins
Boxing Day (Canada and UK)

27 Sunday

2nd ♊
Color: Gold

December/January

28 Monday

2nd ♊
☽ v/c 10:01 pm
Color: Ivory

Rose incense opens the heart to self-love and romance.

☺ Tuesday

2nd ♊
☽ enters ♋ 5:28 am
Full Moon 10:28 pm
Color: Gray

Long Nights Moon

30 Wednesday

3rd ♋
Color: Yellow

31 Thursday

3rd ♋
☽ v/c 8:45 am
☽ enters ♌ 1:58 pm
Color: White

New Year's Eve

1 Friday

3rd ♌
Color: Rose

New Year's Day
Kwanzaa ends

Full Moon in Cancer

We come full circle, as the year is embraced both at the beginning and at its end with the Full Moon in Cancer. We revisit the themes of the sacred feminine, women's issues, nurturing, emotional well-being, family, and home. It is a good time to work magic that honors the Goddess in her many aspects. As the Moon is in her own sign, lunar magic, especially scrying with water, can be especially illuminating. Trust your instincts and intuition. Our emotions can intensify when the Moon is full in Cancer. We are pulled by the undercurrents of memory and the past and may feel nostalgic, sentimental, or melancholy, yearning for a sense of belonging that we can't quite put our finger on. We may feel an overwhelming desire to return "home." This is a good time to gather with family of the heart, those with whom you feel a sense of emotional safety.

Demeter, help me trust the cycles and remember that spring always follows winter.

Guiding Goddesses: Ceres, Holdja, Mother Mary, Taweret

—Danielle Blackwood

---

2 Saturday

3rd ♌
☽ v/c 5:00 pm
☽ enters ♍ 8:13 pm
Color: Indigo

Faumea is an Oceanic creator goddess. Eels are sacred to her.

---

3 Sunday
3rd ♍
Color: Amber

About the Contributors

ELIZABETH BARRETTE was the managing editor of *PanGaia* and has been involved with the Pagan community for more than twenty-five years. Her other writings include speculative fiction and gender studies. Her book *Composing Magic* explains how to write spells, rituals, and other liturgy. She lives in central Illinois and enjoys herbal landscaping and gardening for wildlife. Visit penultimate productions.weebly.com and ysabetwordsmith.dreamwidth.org.

DANIELLE BLACKWOOD has studied and practiced astrology for more than thirty years. As a priestess, she has been facilitating workshops, classes, ceremony, and retreats on astrology and women's mysteries since 1994. Danielle lives in an enchanted cottage on magical Salt Spring Island in the Salish Sea with her husband, Jamie, a six-toed cat named Watson, and a rescue Staffordshire Terrier named Daisy. Visit danielleblackwood.com.

EMILY CARLIN is a Witch, writer, teacher, mediator, and ritual presenter based in Seattle, WA. She currently teaches one-on-one online and at in-person events on the West Coast. For more information and links to her blogs, go to about.me/ecarlin.

ANNA FRANKLIN is an herbalist, a third-degree Witch, and the high priestess of the Hearth of Arianrhod. She's the author of thirty books, including *The Hearth Witch's Kitchen Herbal*, *The Hearth Witch's Compendium*, *The Sacred Circle Tarot*, and *The Fairy Ring Oracle*. Anna has contributed hundreds of articles to Pagan magazines and has appeared on radio and TV. She lives in the UK and can be found online at AnnaFranklin.co.uk.

JENNIFER HEWITSON has been a freelance illustrator since 1985. Her illustrations have appeared in local and national publications, including the *Wall Street*

Journal, the *Washington Post*, the *Los Angeles Times*, *US News & World Report*, and *Ladybug* magazine. Her advertising and packaging clients include Disney and the San Diego Zoo. Jennifer has created a line of greeting cards for Sun Rise Publications and has illustrated several children's books. Her work has been recognized by numerous organizations, including the Society of Illustrators of Los Angeles, and magazines such as *Communication Arts*, *Print*, and *How*.

JAMES KAMBOS studied ancient Middle Eastern civilization in college, which sparked an interest in ancient occult arts and deities. Today he's a writer and artist living in Ohio. He has a degree in history and geography from Ohio University.

At a party someone put a tarot deck in **BARBARA MOORE**'s hands. She's held on tight ever since. In the meantime, Barbara has published quite a few books and decks. She loves cake, art supplies, summer, traveling, and good books, a few of the things that convince Barbara that the Divine loves us and wants us to be happy. Barbara lives in a sunny valley in northern California with her wife. Find her at tarotshaman.com.

MELISSA TIPTON is a licensed massage therapist, Reiki Master, and tarot reader who helps people live more magically through her healing practice, Life Alchemy Massage Therapy. She's the author of *Living Reiki: Heal Yourself and Transform Your Life*, and you can read more of her witchy writing, take online classes, and book tarot readings at getmomassage.com and yogiwitch.com. She loves digging in the garden, getting lost in a pile of books, and hiking with her husband in the woods (aka, looking for faeries).

TESS WHITEHURST teaches magical and intuitive arts in live workshops and via her online community and learning hub, the Good Vibe Tribe Online School of Magical Arts. An award-winning author, she's written eight books, which have been translated into eighteen languages. She's appeared on Bravo, Fox, and NBC, and her writing has been featured in *Writer's Digest*, *Spirit and Destiny* (in the UK), and on her popular website, tesswhitehurst.com.

CHARLIE RAINBOW WOLF is happiest when she is creating something, especially if it can be made from items that others have cast aside. Pottery, writing, knitting, astrology, and tarot are her deepest interests. A recorded singer-songwriter and a published author, she is an advocate of organic gardening and cooking and lives in the Midwest with her husband and special-needs Great Danes. Visit charlierainbow.com.

LAURA TEMPEST ZAKROFF is a professional artist, author, dancer, and has been a practicing Modern Traditional Witch for over two decades. She blogs for Patheos as *A Modern Traditional Witch* and for *Witches & Pagans* as *Fine Art Witchery*, and she contributes to *The Witches' Almanac*. Laura is the author of *Sigil Witchery*, *The Witch's Cauldron*, *The Witch's Altar* (with Jason Mankey), and *Weave the Liminal*. Visit lauratempestzakroff.com.

Appendix

Daily Magical Influences

Each day is ruled by a planet with specific magical influences.

Monday (Moon): peace, healing, caring, psychic awareness
Tuesday (Mars): passion, courage, aggression, protection
Wednesday (Mercury): study, travel, divination, wisdom
Thursday (Jupiter): expansion, money, prosperity, generosity
Friday (Venus): love, friendship, reconciliation, beauty
Saturday (Saturn): longevity, endings, homes
Sunday (Sun): healing, spirituality, success, strength, protection

Color Correspondences

Colors are associated with each day, according to planetary influence.

Monday: gray, lavender, white, silver, ivory
Tuesday: red, white, black, gray, maroon, scarlet
Wednesday: yellow, brown, white, topaz
Thursday: green, turquoise, white, purple, crimson
Friday: white, pink, rose, purple, coral
Saturday: brown, gray, blue, indigo, black
Sunday: yellow, orange, gold, amber

Lunar Phases

Waxing, from New Moon to Full Moon, is the ideal time to do magic to draw things to you.

Waning, from Full Moon to New Moon, is a time for study, meditation, and magical work designed to banish harmful energies.

The Moon's Sign

The Moon continuously moves through each sign of the zodiac, from Aries to Pisces, staying about two and a half days in each sign. The Moon influences the sign it inhabits, creating different energies that affect our day-to-day lives.

Aries: Good for starting things. Things occur rapidly but quickly pass. People tend to be argumentative and assertive.

Taurus: Things begun now last longest, tend to increase in value, and become hard to change. Brings out an appreciation for beauty and sensory experience.

Gemini: Things begun now are easily changed by outside influence. Time for shortcuts, communication, games, and fun.

Cancer: Stimulates emotional rapport between people. Supports growth and nurturing. Tend to domestic concerns.

Leo: Draws emphasis to the self, to central ideas or institutions, away from connections with others and emotional needs.

Virgo: Favors accomplishment of details and commands from higher up. Focus on health, hygiene, and daily schedules.

Libra: Favors cooperation, compromise, social activities, balance, friendship, and partnership.

Scorpio: Increases awareness of psychic power. Precipitates psychic crises and ends connections thoroughly. People have a tendency to brood and become secretive.

Sagittarius: Encourages confidence and flights of imagination. This is an adventurous, philosophical, and athletic Moon sign. Favors expansion and growth.

Capricorn: Develops strong structure. Focus on traditions, responsibilities, and obligations. A good time to set boundaries and rules.

Aquarius: Rebellious energy. Time to break habits and make abrupt change. Personal freedom and individuality is the focus.

Pisces: The focus is on dreaming, nostalgia, intuition, and psychic impressions. A good time for spiritual or philanthropic activities.

Gemstones

Gemstones can be utilized for a variety of purposes and intentions.

Amber: ambition, balance, clarity, healing, protection, success

Amethyst: awareness, harmony, love, spirituality, protection

Citrine: beginnings, change, clarity, goals, goodness, rebirth, sleep

Emerald: clairvoyance, enchantment, jealousy, luck, spirits, wishes

Hematite: balance, grounding, knowledge, negativity, power, strength

Jade: abundance, dream work, money, nurture, peace, well-being, wisdom

Lodestone: attraction, fidelity, grounding, relationships, willpower

Moonstone: destiny, divination, intuition, knowledge, light, sleep

Obsidian: afterlife, aggression, death, fear, grounding, growth, obstacles

Quartz: awareness, clarity, communication, guidance, healing, rebirth

Ruby: compassion, connections, happiness, love, loyalty, passion, respect

Sapphire: astral realm, dedication, emotions, faith, improvement, insight

Tiger's Eye: battle, clarity, desire, energy, purification, strength, youth

Topaz: adaptability, courage, instrospection, loss, prosperity, wisdom

Tourmaline: attraction, business, consciousness, guidance, psychic ability

Turquoise: calm, change, creativity, dream work, empathy, energy, goals, healing, unity

Chakras

Chakras are spiritual energy centers located along the middle of the body.

Root Chakra: Activate with red. Balance with black.
Associated with comfort, grounding, security, support.

Sacral Chakra: Activate with orange. Balance with brown.
Associated with creativity, desire, freedom, passion.

Solar Plexus Chakra: Activate with yellow. Balance with brown.
Associated with confidence, power, transformation, willpower.

Heart Chakra: Activate with green. Balance with pink, rose.
Associated with beauty, compassion, healing, love, mindfulness.

Throat Chakra: Activate with blue. Balance with turquoise.
Associated with communication, inspiration, release, truth.

Forehead Chakra: Activate with indigo. Balance with white.
Associated with clarity, illumination, intuition, visions, wisdom.

Crown Chakra: Activate with violet, purple. Balance with gold, white.
Associated with consciousness, cosmic energy, enlightenment, knowledge, spirituality.

Herbs

Herbs are useful in spells, rituals, cooking and Kitchen Witchery, health, beauty, and crafts and have many common magical correspondences.

Basil: defense, home, love, prosperity, protection, purification, success

Borage: authority, business, happinesss, money, power, purification

Carnation: confidence, creativity, healing, protection, strength, truth

Chamomile: balance, beauty, calm, dream work, gentleness, peace, sleep

Clover: community, friendship, kindness, luck, wealth, youth

Daffodil: afterlife, beauty, faeries, fertility, luck, spirits

Daisy: beauty, cheerfulness, divination, innocence, love, pleasure

Dandelion: awareness, clarity, emotions, freedom, the mind, wishes

Fennel: aggression, courage, energy, stimulation, protection, strength

Fern: banishing, concentration, money, power, protection, release, spirits

Gardenia: comfort, compassion, the home, marriage, peace, true love

Garlic: anxiety, banishing, defense, healing, improvement, weather

Geranium: balance, concentration, fertility, forgiveness, healing

Honeysuckle: affection, gentleness, happiness, optimism, psychic ability

Ivy: animals, attachments, fertility, fidelity, growth, honor, secrets, security

Jasmine: binding, desire, dream work, grace, prosperity, relationships

Lavender: calm, creativity, friendship, peace, purification, sensitivity, sleep

Lilac: adaptability, beauty, clairvoyance, divination, emotions, spirits

Marigold: authority, awareness, endurance, healing, longevity, visions

Marjoram: comfort, family, innocence, loneliness, love, purification

Peppermint: action, awaken, clarity, intelligence, the mind, stimulation

Poppy: astral realm, dream work, fertility, luck, prosperity, sleep, visions

Rose: affection, attraction, blessings, fidelity, love, patience, sexuality

Rosemary: banishing, binding, defense, determination, healing, memory, protection

Sage: consecration, grounding, guidance, memory, obstacles, reversal

Thyme: confidence, growth, happiness, honesty, purification, sorrow

Violet: beauty, changes, endings, heartbreak, hope, lust, passion, shyness

Yarrow: awareness, banishing, calm, challenges, power, protection, success

See *Llewellyn's Complete Book of Correspondences* by Sandra Kynes for a comprehensive catalog of correspondences.

2020 Eclipses

January 10, 2:21 pm; Lunar eclipse 20° ♋ 00'
June 5, 3:12 pm; Lunar eclipse 15° ♐ 34'
June 21, 2:41 am; Solar eclipse 0° ♋ 21'
July 5, 12:44 am; Lunar eclipse 13° ♑ 38'
November 30, 4:30 am; Lunar eclipse 8° ♊ 38'
December 14, 11:17 am; Solar eclipse 23° ♐ 08'

2020 Full Moons

Cold Moon: January 10, 2:21 pm
Quickening Moon: February 9, 2:33 am
Storm Moon: March 9, 1:48 pm
Wind Moon: April 7, 10:35 pm
Flower Moon: May 7, 6:45 am
Strong Sun Moon: June 5, 3:12 pm
Blessing Moon: July 5, 12:44 am
Corn Moon: August 3, 11:59 am
Harvest Moon: September 2, 1:22 am
Blood Moon: October 1, 5:05 pm
Blue Moon: October 31, 10:49 am
Mourning Moon: November 30, 4:30 am
Long Nights Moon: December 29, 10:28 pm

Planetary Retrogrades in 2020

Uranus	℞	08/11/19	10:27 pm	— Direct	01/10/20	8:49 pm
Mercury	℞	02/16/20	7:54 pm	— Direct	03/09/20	11:49 pm
Pluto	℞	04/25/20	2:54 pm	— Direct	10/04/20	9:32 am
Saturn	℞	05/11/20	12:09 am	— Direct	09/29/20	1:11 am
Venus	℞	05/13/20	2:45 am	— Direct	06/25/20	2:48 am
Jupiter	℞	05/14/20	10:32 am	— Direct	09/12/20	8:41 pm
Mercury	℞	06/18/20	12:59 am	— Direct	07/12/20	4:26 am
Neptune	℞	06/23/20	12:31 am	— Direct	11/28/20	7:36 pm
Uranus	℞	08/15/20	10:25 am	— Direct	01/14/21	3:36 am
Mars	℞	09/09/20	6:22 pm	— Direct	11/13/20	7:36 pm
Mercury	℞	10/13/20	9:05 pm	— Direct	11/03/20	12:50 pm

Set in Eastern Time. All times corrected for Daylight Saving Time.

Moon Void-of-Course Data for 2020

Last Aspect		New Sign		
Date	Time	Sign	New Time	

JANUARY

Date	Time	Sign	New Time
1	9:14 pm	1 ♈	11:00 pm
3	8:18 pm	4 ♉	11:15 am
6	7:08 am	6 ♊	9:11 pm
8	5:16 pm	9 ♋	3:43 am
10	6:58 pm	11 ♌	7:16 am
13	8:42 am	13 ♍	9:06 am
15	7:12 am	15 ♎	10:43 am
17	7:58 am	17 ♏	1:20 pm
19	4:22 pm	19 ♐	5:41 pm
20	11:46 pm	22 ♑	12:00 am
23	9:08 pm	24 ♒	8:20 am
25	2:06 pm	26 ♓	6:44 pm
28	8:08 pm	28 ♈	6:51 am
31	10:10 am	31 ♉	7:28 pm

FEBRUARY

Date	Time	Sign	New Time
3	6:28 am	3 ♊	6:29 am
5	9:20 am	5 ♋	2:03 pm
7	10:43 am	7 ♌	5:45 pm
9	11:08 am	9 ♍	6:39 pm
11	1:26 pm	11 ♎	6:37 pm
13	4:40 pm	13 ♏	7:37 pm
15	5:20 pm	15 ♐	11:07 pm
18	4:03 am	18 ♑	5:37 am
20	9:18 am	20 ♒	2:42 pm
21	11:08 pm	23 ♓	1:37 am
25	9:12 am	25 ♈	1:47 pm
27	10:25 pm	28 ♉	2:30 am

MARCH

Date	Time	Sign	New Time
1	10:52 am	1 ♊	2:21 pm
3	9:20 pm	3 ♋	11:25 pm
6	2:11 am	6 ♌	4:27 am
8	4:12 am	8 ♍	6:47 am
10	4:32 am	10 ♎	6:03 am
12	4:12 am	12 ♏	5:28 am
14	6:06 am	14 ♐	7:09 am
16	5:34 am	16 ♑	12:25 pm
18	8:48 pm	18 ♒	9:16 pm
20	5:00 am	21 ♓	8:33 am
23	10:51 am	23 ♈	8:58 pm
26	3:16 am	26 ♉	9:37 am
28	7:05 pm	28 ♊	9:38 pm
30	11:10 am	31 ♋	7:43 am

APRIL

Date	Time	Sign	New Time
2	12:49 pm	2 ♌	2:26 pm
3	3:29 pm	4 ♍	5:18 pm
6	9:29 am	6 ♎	5:16 pm
8	8:50 am	8 ♏	4:17 pm
10	3:35 pm	10 ♐	4:35 pm
12	7:46 am	12 ♑	8:05 pm
14	7:47 pm	15 ♒	3:37 am
17	10:34 am	17 ♓	2:29 pm
19	7:31 pm	20 ♈	3:00 am
22	8:32 am	22 ♉	3:36 pm
24	8:43 pm	25 ♊	3:20 am
27	1:00 pm	27 ♋	1:28 pm
29	3:29 pm	29 ♌	9:06 pm

MAY

Date	Time	Sign	New Time
1	12:04 pm	2 ♍	1:35 am
3	10:25 pm	4 ♎	3:09 am
5	10:31 pm	6 ♏	3:05 am
7	10:39 pm	8 ♐	3:15 am
10	2:11 pm	10 ♑	5:39 am
12	6:30 am	12 ♒	11:39 am
14	10:03 am	14 ♓	9:24 pm
17	3:59 am	17 ♈	9:36 am
19	4:33 pm	19 ♉	10:10 pm
22	4:01 am	22 ♊	9:36 am
24	7:09 am	24 ♋	7:09 pm
26	9:06 pm	27 ♌	2:33 am
28	9:30 am	29 ♍	7:40 am
31	5:17 am	31 ♎	10:38 am

JUNE

Date	Time	Sign	New Time
2	6:40 am	2 ♏	12:06 pm
4	7:36 am	4 ♐	1:17 pm
6	12:10 am	6 ♑	3:44 pm
8	2:06 pm	8 ♒	8:54 pm
10	10:35 am	11 ♓	5:32 am
13	8:35 am	13 ♈	5:03 pm
15	8:49 am	16 ♉	5:35 am
18	8:02 am	18 ♊	5:00 pm
20	5:48 pm	21 ♋	2:02 am
23	3:20 am	23 ♌	8:33 am
24	1:34 am	25 ♍	1:05 pm
27	4:02 pm	27 ♎	4:16 pm
29	9:02 am	29 ♏	6:48 pm

JULY

Date	Time	Sign	New Time
1	9:20 pm	1 ♐	9:21 pm
3	9:06 am	4 ♑	12:48 am
5	5:35 am	6 ♒	6:08 am
7	12:37 am	8 ♓	2:13 pm
10	11:49 pm	11 ♈	1:06 am
13	11:54 am	13 ♉	1:34 pm
15	11:21 pm	16 ♊	1:19 am
17	5:14 pm	18 ♋	10:24 am
20	1:55 pm	20 ♌	4:16 pm
21	8:27 pm	22 ♍	7:40 pm
24	7:08 pm	24 ♎	9:54 pm
26	9:09 pm	27 ♏	12:12 am
29	12:01 am	29 ♐	3:25 am
30	8:08 pm	31 ♑	7:58 am

AUGUST

Date	Time	Sign	New Time
2	9:59 am	2 ♒	2:11 pm
4	5:45 am	4 ♓	10:28 pm
7	8:53 am	7 ♈	9:05 am
9	3:50 pm	9 ♉	9:28 pm
12	3:55 am	12 ♊	9:46 am
14	7:19 am	14 ♋	7:35 pm
16	7:59 pm	17 ♌	1:38 am
19	1:38 am	19 ♍	4:20 am
20	11:37 pm	21 ♎	5:16 am
23	12:20 am	23 ♏	6:16 am
25	2:27 am	25 ♐	8:49 am
27	8:00 am	27 ♑	1:37 pm
29	3:31 am	29 ♒	8:37 pm

SEPTEMBER

Date	Time	Sign	New Time
1	12:56 am	1 ♓	5:34 am
3	10:34 am	3 ♈	4:22 pm
6	12:45 am	6 ♉	4:43 am
8	8:47 am	8 ♊	5:28 pm
11	12:48 am	11 ♋	4:23 am
13	8:05 am	13 ♌	11:32 am
15	11:09 am	15 ♍	2:37 pm
17	7:42 am	17 ♎	2:56 pm
19	10:29 am	19 ♏	2:33 pm
21	2:13 pm	21 ♐	3:32 pm
23	1:31 pm	23 ♑	7:16 pm
25	11:36 pm	26 ♒	2:08 am
28	3:18 am	28 ♓	11:34 am
30	1:30 pm	30 ♈	10:47 pm

OCTOBER

Date	Time	Sign	New Time
3	1:47 am	3 ♉	11:12 am
5	2:41 pm	6 ♊	12:03 am
7	9:57 pm	8 ♋	11:45 am
10	12:04 am	10 ♌	8:24 pm
12	10:29 am	13 ♍	12:56 am
14	6:47 pm	15 ♎	1:54 am
16	6:11 pm	17 ♏	1:05 am
18	5:43 pm	19 ♐	12:43 am
20	11:38 pm	21 ♑	2:44 am
23	12:35 am	23 ♒	8:17 am
24	5:54 pm	25 ♓	5:18 pm
28	8:46 pm	28 ♈	4:45 am
30	12:12 am	30 ♉	5:19 pm

NOVEMBER

Date	Time	Sign	New Time
1	9:29 pm	2 ♊	5:00 am
4	8:49 am	4 ♋	4:45 pm
6	8:27 pm	7 ♌	2:18 am
9	6:05 am	9 ♍	8:30 am
11	5:58 am	11 ♎	11:09 am
13	6:32 am	13 ♏	11:19 am
15	6:13 am	15 ♐	10:47 am
17	2:55 pm	17 ♑	11:35 am
19	11:30 am	19 ♒	3:25 pm
20	7:49 pm	21 ♓	11:06 pm
24	5:44 am	24 ♈	10:05 am
26	6:46 pm	26 ♉	10:43 pm
29	7:48 am	29 ♊	11:16 am
30	11:22 pm	12/1 ♋	10:33 pm

DECEMBER

Date	Time	Sign	New Time
4	5:29 am	4 ♌	7:53 am
5	5:28 pm	6 ♍	2:46 pm
8	5:35 pm	8 ♎	7:01 pm
10	7:56 pm	10 ♏	8:59 pm
12	8:58 pm	12 ♐	9:39 pm
14	11:17 am	14 ♑	10:35 pm
17	12:34 am	17 ♒	1:27 am
19	3:45 am	19 ♓	7:39 am
21	5:25 am	21 ♈	5:32 pm
23	5:51 pm	24 ♉	5:55 am
26	6:32 am	26 ♊	6:33 pm
28	10:01 pm	29 ♋	5:28 am
31	5:45 am	31 ♌	1:58 pm

Set in Eastern Time. All times corrected for Daylight Saving Time.

Notes

Notes

Notes